ROAD SIGNS

To Guide You Along Your Professional Journey

Powerful Insights from a Veteran Start Up Evangelist
and Business Advisor

Written & Edited by

PRANAB K. PANI

INDIA · SINGAPORE · MALAYSIA

Notion Press Media Pvt Ltd

No. 50, Chettiyar Agaram Main Road,
Vanagaram, Chennai, Tamil Nadu – 600 095

First Published by Notion Press 2021
Copyright © Pranab K. Pani 2021
All Rights Reserved.

ISBN
Hardcase 978-1-68523-476-8
Paperback 978-1-68523-426-3

DEDICATION

This book is dedicated to all the beautiful young minds entering into the corporate world and starting their professional career with dreams and aspirations. May you build up a strong nation while building your careers and characters. Let knowledge and wisdom rule this world and people share love and compassion.

And,

To my beloved Late Parents and my Gods, Smt. Harapriya Pani and Sri Judhisthir Pani – who had taught their children all the good things that every parent does, while instilling values but urged us to strive to be good human beings first. My respected father was the one who encouraged me constantly to express myself through writing, thrusting the pen between my nimble fingers and constantly telling me that knowledge is the only weapon that would give me respect and a dignified identity. My love for the Queen's tongue grew stronger only because of him. I owe everything to my dear father, who always prided him with everything that I used to do, though we exchanged fewer words in between. This book is my humble homage to my dear Baba.

CONTENTS

FOREWORD

DR. KIRAN MAZUMDAR-SHAW

Executive Chairperson, BIOCON Biologics,
Bangalore, India

We are living in the most exciting and best of times ever in terms of the potential we have to change the world with the help of technology. We are witnessing the birth of technologies that will fundamentally alter the way we live, work, and relate to one another. The scale, scope, and complexity of the transformation is unlikely to be like anything humankind has experienced before.

The first three Industrial Revolutions have seen the displacement and disruption of businesses by locomotives, electricity and computers. Now a Fourth Industrial Revolution is underway wherein technologies are converging to blur the lines between the physical, digital, and biological spheres.

Compared with previous industrial revolutions, the Fourth is evolving at an exponential rather than a linear pace. Moreover, it is disrupting almost every industry in every country.

At the same time, India is fast emerging as a global technology hub. The country is welcoming investments from the world's leading companies, which is resulting in a vibrant technology sector where international and Indian players, from startups to large MNCs, are looking to make a mark.

We are also witnessing the entry of a vast number of millennials into the workforce. Millennials also known as the Generation Y, born between 1980 and 2000, are expected to account for roughly 75% of the global workforce by 2025.

This vibrancy is fuelling India's socioeconomic development and becoming a defining pillar of India's lauded identity and ambition on the international stage.

It is in this context that *Pranab K. Pani's* anthology of essays, **Road Signs**, offers interesting insights into subjects as diverse as Start-ups, Disruptive Innovation, Human Resource Development, Managing Change, E-Commerce, Social Behaviour, Workplace Stress, Leadership as well as, Millennials of the Digital Age.

It comprises 22 select articles written by the author, who is a corporate veteran and an entrepreneur today, while being a mentor to several start-ups in India.

Pani draws on his decades of experience in the corporate world to provide rare insights into the changing nature of the world we live in and how to make sense of the change.

This book is a must-read for the youth of today who are looking for 'road signs' to shape their professional careers even as they aspire to reshape the future.

ACKNOWLEDGEMENTS

I acknowledge with gratitude:

My good senior friends, well-wishers and all my dear family members:

Dr. (Mrs.) Kiran Mazumdar-Shaw ma'am for being so encouraging and kind in her words, while writing the Foreword in my book, which is like a tiara to my writings.

The acclaimed Poet & Author, Commodore (Retd) Dillip Mohapatra VSM, for volunteering to review this book and christened it appropriately as "Road Signs".

And several of you dear learned friends and respected seniors, who have encouraged me constantly to express myself fearlessly and share knowledge through my pen and talks.

And Yes of course, to my Better-half Mrs. Pragnya Pani aka Mita, for being patient with my continuous writings and public talks while tolerating my time away from the family in social service. She's a great support, strength and a critic, wanting me always to be more realistic and grounded. And Kumar Aditya (Guddu), our Son, has been a great hope and true love in our life, which helps me in my positive thoughts and faith in today's youth.

And to my respected dear elder Brother (Muna Bhaina) Sri Pradipta Kishore Pani and my beloved elder Sister (Runu Nani) Smt. Namita Panda for their love and encouragement all through.

The speed and agility of my enterprising nephew Prem Prakash Pani (Vicky) got this book seeing the light of the day, joining hands with the Notion Press on his recommendation and push. This helped me getting my manuscript a tangible shape, to be available to you all my readers, the youth especially...moving from the college to the corporate.

MILLENNIALS OF THE DIGITAL AGE

World is home to 1.8 billion young people between the ages 10-20 years and quite a large population of them live in less developed countries.

With 356 million 10-24 year olds, India has the world's largest youth population. Nearly 41 percent of the population in India is below 24 years old. The following countries follow India in the same respectively. China – 269 million, Indonesia – 67 million, US – 65 million, Pakistan – 59 million, Nigeria – 57 million, Brazil – 51 million and Bangladesh – 48 million. It's also predicted that by 2020 India will be home to 64% youths of its population.

"Today's young people live in a highly connected but non-physical world."

This offers enormous opportunities to transform the future. The potential gains would be realized through a "demographic dividend", which can occur when a country's working age population is larger than the population that is dependent on.

Young people are innovators, creators, builders and leaders of the future. But they can benefit from the future only if they have skills, health, decision-making ability, and real choices in life. Changes occur and a country marches ahead when its youth leads and remains active in all spheres of life.

Traditionally, the youth rebels, questions the status quo, prefers razzmatazz to plain vanilla and is, fashion conscious and career minded.

The world is growing young and a huge number of young aspirational souls move about with thoughts and actions different from the ones followed by the earlier generations. There is a marked difference in their approach to life that manifests in their daily activities, their likes and dislikes.

Today's young people live in a highly connected but non-physical world. Gen-Y is tech-savvy, open minded, narcissist, vanity, selfish, opinionated, impatient and fiercely independent. They are a disenchanted lot as well... the dogmatic society with its rituals and the preaching seniors disinterest them. The world they dream of, espouse and very vocal about, centers around a playful self-centric yet very pragmatic canvas that lives beyond any geographical and religious boundaries. They are an aspirational lot who pride in nationalism at the same time, advocate universal brotherhood. They are adventurous and don't hesitate to experiment the alien and the new. These traits imbibe in them an exploratory mind, which delves into the mystic elements as well unravel scientific treasures. They believe in what they see and experience. Hard-nosed politicians and divisive vote-bank politics don't appeal them.

They evoke a contrarian picture as well...selfish yet compassionate, impulsive yet calculative, impatient yet dogged with their pursuit, fun loving, jovial & playful yet concerned about nature, environment, love eating packaged snacks, drinks and junk food yet health conscious and gym regulars. Born with electronic gadgets around and playing with the same, they develop scientific temperament and are naturally attracted to anything that keeps them engaged in that line. No wonder, video games, mobile phones and cartoons are their staple pastime and inseparable from them. They believe in working smart and enjoying harder. Born to consumerism and in a highly materialistic world, over indulgence and a penchant for hedonism come natural to today's youth. Even the smart marketers take advantage of their mindset cater to their whims and fancies. Today's youth live in the fast lane and patience wears thin on them. Instant gratification is desired and loved. They are attention seekers look forward to being appreciated and applauded.

Loath them or find fault in them, you can't ignore them. They are the future of the country and it surely pays to understand them and join hands with them in creating a world that they aspire for and aim at. Gen-Y is paying the price for the baby boomers who now are retirees and pensioners. Old order changes yielding to the new. The demographic dividend would become a huge

"Today's young force is epitome of hope offering plenty of possibilities that need to be supported with imagination and sincerity. The overflowing raw energy must get channelized in the right direction with positivity and purpose."

liability if this large young force is neglected and the realities don't meet their aspirations. They are a potential force who could transform this world to a better place to live in and enjoy about. They also could be potentially dangerous if they fall into the hands of negative elements with radical idealism. We all are witness to this disturbing side as well. Narrow minded and self-serviced politicians, radical ideologists and fundamentalists could mold them dangerously which could pose a grave threat to the world and its population. Social scientists are quite concerned at this possibility and are justifiably disturbed at the unfortunate developments across the world. Fear lurks in the mind when talents and youthful energies are misused. Social media is being used and manipulated to gain rebel support and modulating public opinion with a pernicious motive. Today's youth is being used towards this. This is posing a grave challenge to the world leaders and social scientists. The silver lining in this hovering dark cloud is a welcome surge in entrepreneurship with innovation and a growing effort at solving problems in the world though technology. This not only diverts the trend towards generating employment and creating jobs but helps the mankind and bridges the gap between the demand and the supply with plenty to choose from.

Today's youth force is epitome of hope offering plenty of possibilities that need to be supported with imagination and sincerity. The overflowing raw energy must get channelized in the right direction with positivity and purpose.

In order to maximize the dividend, countries must ensure their young working-age populations are equipped with the desired knowledge, skills and attitudes to seize opportunities for jobs and other income-earning possibilities, the UN agency said in one of its recent reports.

When the youth sings, "we're the world", we all must join them and be with them rather than looking down upon painting them all in the same brush. India must seize the opportunity for its benefit and lead the world. Advantage Young India. Together WE Can!

MEDIA AND THE YOUTH

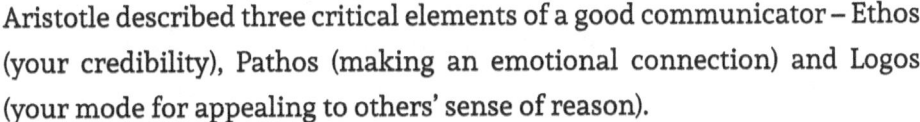

Aristotle described three critical elements of a good communicator – Ethos (your credibility), Pathos (making an emotional connection) and Logos (your mode for appealing to others' sense of reason).

With the advent of technology, mankind today is experiencing a media onslaught. Television has made inroads into our living rooms bringing in news & features from across the globe. The globe has shrunk today with the ubiquitous presence of all pervading Internet – world-wide-web! Information is made available at the click of a button, in the palmtop. News spreads faster than sound. The various mobile devices including the wireless mobile phones get up everything on the move. Well, science & technology is

"The baton is always passed down from the elders. It is imperative that youth may rely on the rich experience and knowledge of the older generation, but fresh breath of ideas and leadership could bring in quality youth movement. This is acutely desired in the fields of Communication and PR world."

constantly innovating to keep pace with the demanding aspirations and work requirements of evolved humankind. We are spoilt for choice. The aim is to make life simpler and comfortable. But, the choice is yours, how you use them, and for what purpose.

Writer Anthony Downs in his essay "Up & Down with Ecology – the issue attention cycle" in a 1972 issue of "The Public Interest" – an American journal that is still relevant, wrote "Public attention towards any important issue tends to rise and fall in five distinct stages." He further elaborates that "news is consumed by the public and is a form of entertainment. As such it competes with other types of entertainment for a share of each person's time." Now this is the challenge the media is experiencing in the 21st century and hence, the means adopted. Today the media not only tries for better TRP rate to stay afloat and commercially viable among competition but also fights hard this growing changing audience taste.

One thing is quite apparent here that today's youth is more informative. This impacts her personality and psyche. When things move faster and everything gets obsolete in no time, this has influenced today's youth as well. The often cited 'attention deficit' and 'instant gratification' are borne out of this rapid changing world. Now this is the biggest challenge that the media as well as the social scientists are facing with.

The simmering clamour for validation unleashes the exhibitionism streak. This manifests our social behaviour as could be seen in various social networks. This allows us to talk behind cloaked profile. Even an introvert expresses herself to everything that she may not speak up in front of you. More often than not our expressions find constant response and many a times, cynical support and even gratifying moments for the attention seekers, egg us onto more self-indulgent. There is an issue attention cycle in the age of artificial excitement and overpowering cynicism.

Convergent media gives massive speed and access to information but much of media news is lifted up from social media without validation. Accountability becomes nil. People express their apprehension of crash commercialization in media. The credibility, objectivity and fairness get compromised at every level while reporting. The disturbing trend of 'paid news' camouflaging as reporting news and certain media houses aligning with powers that be, destroys the ethical morale of the fourth estate. Many a newspaper and TV channel resort to sensationalism and cooked up stories to win more eye balls and advertisement revenues. This is very dangerous to the democracy and to the society in general. This is misuse of power. Media most of the times influences general public thinking and logic particularly in a still developing and poverty stricken country like India. Several media houses are also owned by business houses having allegiance to certain political party and faith group. Relaying and transmitting news and analysis gets influenced at times. Offering of biased and one-sided stories could not only distort the truth but could mislead the audience, creating a conflicting situation.

The informed youth of today need to be alert at all developments around and should use its rational thinking ability without getting opinionated or swayed away by vested news. This requires a broad sensibility and all inclusive approach. Tolerance towards different faith, culture and language is required. Agreeing to disagree is very important as well in conflicting views and issues. It's easy said than done but better assessment with respect to other view-points would lessen the looming discord. Leadership is important, neither you should be pushed around nor taken for granted. A conscious, alert, considerate and responsible youth leader could save the nation from its brink. Youth are the epitome of courage and innovation. This quality assumes significance in a democratic set up, particularly when the majority of the population is still below the poverty line with less education and awareness. This great nation needs more of Vivekanandas, spreading the real values of life and inspiring, accountable leadership. The baton is always passed down from the elders. It is imperative that youth may rely on the rich experience and knowledge of the older generation, but fresh breath of ideas and leadership could bring in quality youth movement. This is acutely desired in the fields of Communication and PR world.

It is very interesting to observe the trend in the users of social media and their penchant for publicity and endorsement. If one analyses Facebook, one would find a disturbing streak of narcissism and exhibitionism. This reflects on the contemporary social milieu and human behaviour. This public platform provides an outlet to even the most introverts, expressing self brazenly. The inclusive democracy of the social media allows the marginalised user to give opinions and to make statements emotively. Of course, an unbridled opinion would create strife in the society but nevertheless, empowers ordinary folks to opine and react.

Democratization of Media would help - Working with information and media consumers for increasing access to media, creating intimate media among media consumers to support peer groups in spreading media literacy, developing indicators to self-measure impact and outcomes of such efforts.

Building and operating experimental media, supporting autonomous media should be the efforts of today's youth. They also need close Liaison with mainstream media for progressive media and information policies and research into mainstream media policies for identifying gaps and opportunities. In other words Policy Intervention-Research, Debates and Discussions about media policies of the government, firms, institutions and media firms would help improving the situation.

With power comes responsibility and media has to remember this. It definitely helps influencing opinions and winds of change. This powerful tool needs to be used effectively, prudently and with care. Misuse of this overtly or through covert means would destroy and destabilize the society. Youth should guard against this and should strive to be alert and responsible citizen.

- The number of followers in Facebook would constitute third populated country in the world. There are about 300 million photos posted on this daily.

- After revolutionizing the digital consumer market with its innovative iPod and iPhones, Apple Inc under the visionary leadership of the late Steve Jobs introduced iPad in April 2010. This completely changed the way we use computer and changed the rules in the industry.

- Every year India produces about 3,60,000 Engineering Graduates, about 6 lakhs general graduates, about 5000 PhDs.

- Only 25% of engineering Graduates, 10% general graduates and about 100 PhDs are employable! (as per McKinsey report).

- By 2030, 590 million people in India will live in cities, nearly twice the population of USA today.

- By 2030 about 91 million urban households will be middleclass. Up from 22 million today.

- By 2030, 68 cities will have population of 1 million plus, up from 42 today. Europe has only 35 today.

- There are 47 million Credit cards and 924 million Debit Cards users in India with 3.7 million POS and 225,000 ATMs in India.

- India's largest digital payment company Paytm has 12 million payment merchants, 47 million Paytm bank savings account, 94 million KYC wallets and 371 million total Paytm users....and growing faster.

Changes are the order of the day and constant truth in a developing country and progressive world. All pervasive presence of different modes and types of media would surely impact the society. The culture and mindset all changes along with it. The youth today has a powerful medium available free to express; responsible communication and restrained emotion would help. Both are still evolving. Hope, the going forward would be a matured journey together.

INDIA'S UNEMPLOYABLE ENGINEERING GRADUATES

Tech Mahindra CEO Mr. CP Gurnani says that nearly 94% Engineering Graduates are Unemployable!

The problem

As I understand, this problem is two pronged:

1. Colleges are not making their students Industry Ready and not Skilling them with Industry demanded Tech Skills. Rather, focusing only on the Campus Selection as its tool for business growth and market credibility. It's observed that most of the students are very poor in their Communication skills (Business Communication in particular) as well.

2. Industries can't shirk their responsibilities either. Most IT companies are Sweat Shops/Body shops, focusing only on their business Bottom-line. How many are into Product Development and R&D? IT Services are relatively low-end jobs globally that mostly survive on Low-cost, which is not a sustainable business model in the long run as has been observed. This is why; most Indian companies are struggling today, when world's largest IT

market - USA blocks their entries. How many are having Patents? What is the industry doing to equip and update these students with the latest technologies, supporting the academic?

There's another dimension to it as well i.e. the quality of the Teachers. They fail to go that extra mile to take ownership of the students and pride in their works. Life skills are not being taught either, making the young minds weak while facing challenges in life. They're unable to accept defeat and rejections. Most of these teachers are themselves not fully versed with the newer technologies.

When China is building Centres of Excellence, India is introducing Reservations in academics and jobs. Merit takes a back seat in Indian polity. The demographic dividend loses steam as the aspiring youth is jobless!

A veteran Engineering Consultant says, being working in the Aircraft industry for over four decades, taking innumerable interviews for recruiting engineers for the industry, the unemployable percentage of the engineers will be more than 94%. Where are the good dedicated teachers? For learning, both the teacher and student should have interest to learn. After passing out from engineering colleges those who do not get job anywhere, go for teaching. What will you expect from them when they themselves are not qualified and without exposure to the industry? You are talking about Academia industry collaboration. Recently he wrote to IIT Bhubaneswar Dean and volunteered himself to impart some courses what industry wants. There was not even an acknowledgment as they remain busy in campus selection.

"The Accredited agencies put emphasis on research and in order to get good rankings, large educational institutes have focused more on research rather than teaching. This has an adverse impact on the education learning."

During my corporate years, I had the similar experiences with the recruitment. Yes, we don't expect them to have Work Experience but the knowledge of what the Industry operates on. Yes, the attitude of the people in the Academics is not so encouraging either. Unfortunately, the Private Corporate and the Private Colleges are mostly centred on the growth of the Top and Bottom Lines. Where will that leave any room for the holistic development of the poor students? I've been receiving offers from several Colleges from many States, asking only for getting them foreign students and help them in Campus Recruitment. No one is interested to engage me professionally as an Industry Representative to bridge the gap with the Academics.

Everyone wants to have a pie of the good times. Volume kills the quality. Here, the first culprits are the Colleges, not keeping pace with the fast changing technologies and churning out Engineering Graduates with out-dated skills. The Industry simply cribs but doesn't come forward to collaborate with the Academics to impart training in the industry Practices and market demands. Students and their parents are happy with the Placements and look forward to "foreign" postings. The vacuum continues unabated. This is the problem with most developing countries in the world. During my visits to these countries and while interacting with the students and teachers there, I hear the same story. Hence, some of us have to come forward to take the cudgels and help arresting the tide. I'm game for this.

Educational institutes need to rethink and develop a new approach to sustain both teaching and research. Four pillars of knowledge in an academic institute include Teaching, Research, Training and Consultancy. The Accredited agencies put emphasis on research and in order to get good rankings, large educational institutes have focused more on research rather than teaching. This has an adverse impact on the education learning. Several teachers are publishing papers that do not add to the body of knowledge. They publish papers to get promotions, as preference is given to the teachers, boasting of more paper publication and books in their CVs. Teachers are also seen to be resorting to certain fake journals. Unlike in the developed countries, research by the teachers in India does not get funded by the industry. Most private colleges do not even pay the UGC Scale to the teachers. Every year 1.5 million engineering students come out of all engineering colleges across India, while the IITs have only 10,000 seats.

Other Challenges:

a.   Dearth of Study Content

b.   Annual Refresher Programme in Testing (ARPIT) for the Higher Education Institutes (HEI) using the SWAYAM platform for online professional development of 1.5 million faculties. Only 0.5% of teachers (5478) attempted online exams under ARPIT scheme. 75 National Resource Centres (NRC) were established for developing online courses in different disciplines.

Time is ripe to have Academia-Industry Collaboration.

Suggested Solutions

The gap analysis would point at the absence of Market and Industry Knowledge and Practices among the students and the teachers. The required skillsets in the prevailing industry is completely absent from the course curriculum, posing serious challenges at the entry level, questioning their employability. Time is ripe to have Academia-Industry Collaboration.

In course of a discussion initiated and moderated by myself on this issue, several corporate professionals, academicians, thought leaders shared their thoughts and observations while offering suggestions as well. While compiling these together, I have used the

"A. Linking the National Colleges with the Local Communities and Towns and B. Industry promoted Innovation and R&D, catering to this local market that could mitigate the problems faced in these places and that could arrest the flight of the Engineers to the Cities. Social Entrepreneurship is the answer to this that could surely help improving the matter in the country"

analytical route to disseminate the same and put them across with my understanding.

There was an interesting suggestion that caught my attention and it says: A. Linking the National Colleges with the Local Communities and Towns and B. Industry promoted Innovation and R&D, catering to this local market that could mitigate the problems faced in these places and that could arrest the flight of the Engineers to the Cities. Social Entrepreneurship is the answer to this that could surely help improving the matter in the country, any country for that matter but the economics of this has to be worked out to sustain interest and living.

IIT Delhi has been working on technologies for rural development. Companies need to step in to commercialize the solution. Similarly, KIIT-TBI and Amrita Incubation encourages and supports with incubation facilities along with seed capital to the start-ups working on solutions in the Social Entrepreneurship. The government needs to provide the enabling environment and incentives. Alas, we are limited by short-term goals, corruption and thinking in siloes (at least that has been the experience when working in rural areas). The 'ideal' scenario is the only scenario worth striving for; otherwise we are forever stuck in the status quo. Certain young professionals are working on a social entrepreneurship solution to connect universities and rural communities to co-develop off-grid renewable energy solutions. They hope to bring green training skills and prepare the future generations in skills for emerging technologies - IoT, 3D printing and AI - with a focus on innovative energy access.

Not everything has to rally around these recently emerging technologies: AI, ML and BC. Of course, they're today all pervasive and widely used, which the Industry has realised of late. Yes, colleges should implement them in their curriculum immediately. But, this won't plug the leaks that we're discussing here. The malaise needs to be tackled holistically and not just with these recently emerged technologies but towards making the students Industry Ready. And for that, it's not just the knowledge and skills in the market driven technology but in other allied subjects as well for a complete package. Indian PM's judicious advice is simply riding on the current development but won't address the problem afflicting the entire education system. We are and should focus on that only. Unfortunately, Education and Healthcare continued to receive scant attention in India from the successive governments. There is no long-term vision to build a robust structure towards creating and developing knowledge economy.

A veteran Aircraft Design Engineer offers his views through his experience with engineering graduates. "We do not expect the fresh graduate to know everything. During interview we try to judge whether the candidate has aptitude to learn. Most of the candidates fail in this. They do not know where to look into for enhancing their required knowledge what industries want. They should go and check with Google or YouTube in the internet. Sincere effort is required to learn and enhance knowledge and skills at all times. Next are our engineering professors, he continues. "I shall give a technical example in aircraft design. They will teach them whole strength of materials writing lengthy equations but will not tell where these equations are used to design an aircraft. They should give a practical example of an aircraft component and teach how it can be used. This is what industries want. When the teachers themselves do not have initiative to find why blame student."

More pertinent question is how we can in our respective roles enable this to happen. I know of an outreach programme Nestle has done to bridge this gap. It's an engagement programme undertaken with select universities of the country where managers from Nestle get involved in training students at the university to increase their skill levels and make them more industry-pertinent. Nirma University is doing the same. It is piloted now and they might increase the number of institution partners based on the feedback and impact.

Indian tech companies run on cost arbitrage rather than innovation. If the primary lever of improving revenue is on cheap labour, spending money on that is an added cost which will erase the top line and mid line of their balance sheet. Instead, they (All tech firms) recycle the workforce by removing redundant positions and hire new resources as per market needs. It is a quick fix but not a long term solution.

I am not sure if the intent is missing. This might not be a priority. Plus it doesn't come at a huge cost. I tend to believe industry per se, has at least some leaders, inspired to make a difference. A humble start can sow the seeds for a huge difference. Perhaps, we can do our part in influencing and getting the balls rolling.

This challenge is not going to end unless we tackle the roots. Quick fix methods will not work when the student has already completed his graduation. Strengthening academics at the early stages with good support from parents, and Teachers along with life skills, love and security can do wonders. No quick fix solutions will work.

True, nothing can replace proper skills. Just a few points: 1) Good education, both schooling & higher, where actual emphasis is given to the practical knowledge rather than just theoretical. That's the difference in literacy & education in real sense. 2) Employers have to factor in the cost of training & developing individuals as expecting a finished product mayn't be practical in long term. In fact, in UK a lot of encouragement is given to apprenticeship programs which trains very young, less educated but good IQ students to achieve skills in particular fields. This also includes getting educated with degrees & diplomas while one works. So, one is a student & worker at the same time. Long term benefits include loyalty, specific skill banks & low cost. 3) Creating an overall environment of knowledge & developments rather than just grades & degrees. Our society is obsessed with percentages, entrances & formal education & hence the outcome is what we see. We should rather tap on the potential of individuals & make them self-belief that they are special & groom them accordingly.

I believe the problem highlighted is a problem we have been hearing since last decade or even more. Most important is, what action is taken by the education institutions, students themselves and Corporates? Business Communication skill is still the biggest gap but problem lies elsewhere. Three fourth students feel they are having English skills or it's not relevant, Colleges think of Business Communication skill importance but only at the later stage and Corporates keep on shrinking Business Communication Programs saying it's an operation burden for them to have more days of training. Even though almost all schools are having English Language Labs but are they working? The products are low cost and not technology proven that could improve the Business Communication Language skills. Language Labs are mere a piece of marketing campaign to extract parents' money. The problem remains a problem if Students, Teachers, Schools, Universities and Corporate do not take enough responsibility and take a measure of the problem. Few odd Universities and Students have now moved towards better English Language Technology enabled personalized learning Solutions in India and Philippines. However we need better strategy to deal with it.

No piecemeal approach could solve this problem in our educational institutions and in the Industry. This requires the collaboration of all concerned stakeholders viz; the Academics, the Industry, the Teachers and the Parents, not to ignore to keep the awareness among the students. But this exercise has to be introduced from the High School level. Yes, Communication in general and Business Communication in particular are the Achilles heel of the students who, in the absence of awareness coupled with an insincere approach of the Academics, that's divorced from the industry Practices, don't help the cause, leaving the Graduates cutting a sorry figure in the Corporate. In my visits to various colleges and universities across India as a Management Speaker and as an Entrepreneur, I stress on this but more often than not, receive a lukewarm response. The College Management doesn't care much about improving this and they continue to churn out less prepared graduates. To my utter shock, in one of the written communication tests for two different popular private college faculties, this author was horrified to notice abysmal quality in the language, mostly with spelling mistakes and grammatical errors. What could one expect these teachers to teach their students?

I think there are two more major attributes to this problem. The first is the courses don't keep pace with the latest discovery. Unlike engineering, the Doctors better update themselves on the latest developments in their field of expertise and in fact put the new technique to use within a reasonable period. But with due respect to Engineering profession, such approach is very rarely observed in day today operation of the field engineer. Another important aspect is the quality of faculty most private colleges maintain. I know quite a few members of the faculty in several colleges, who were anything but average students even. Not only that, they go on to complete their M.Tech! With such teachers, it doesn't require any expertise to imagine the kind of engineers the institutes could churn off. As rightly said, technical education can't and shouldn't be a stand-alone affair. It can't afford to lose sight of the industry. Collaboration between the two will be a case of complimentary catalysing and create a win-win situation both for industry and academics.

With due respect to our teaching fraternity, I can state from experience and knowledge that most Engineering and even B-Schools have the faculties, less knowledgeable and experienced in the changing technologies. Glaring absence of any practical knowledge and experience of the industry operations and market practices on the part of the teachers in the colleges, make the situation worse for the students. More than this is the disturbing statistics of attitudinal issues. Absence of commitment to the job and indulging in Individual research activities, have surely affected the students. That Ownership, as was pointed out earlier, is sorely lacking in most of the teachers today.

Certain private Engineering Universities/Colleges have collaborated with specific organisations in enabling career-ready formal higher education in India. It strives to strengthen 'employability quotient' across the complete spectrum of adult learning - from colleges to corporate.

If Medical studies have been systematic and keeping pace with the changed scenario in this field and producing quality Doctors, why the same could not be emulated by the Engineering academics?

Job Market & Opportunity

On the issue of why the market is not creating enough jobs for the students:

But when the available positions can't be filled up due to this problem and with such gap between the demand and supplies that the complaining Industry is battling with, it's difficult to expect more opportunities, what with the AI and Robotics shrinking the job market further.

Ÿ Michael Brown, CEO at Symantec says that the demand for cyber security professionals is set to increase and can reach up to 6 million job openings by the year 2021. This will lead to a projected short fall of 1.5 million professionals. Ÿ R. Chandrasekhar, NASSCOM President in a recent statement said that, "the estimate is that India has just about 50,000 cyber security professionals; we need at least one million skilled people in this domain by 2021.

Engineering degree does not come cheap. It costs about Rs. 10-15 lakhs (USD 14,000+). For poor parents, it is a huge burden. When their sons and daughters do not secure jobs, it's a devastating experience for them. For the nation, you can calculate the loss. Leave aside the 1 lakh

"Today the situation is that most engineers are working in a field that has no connection to what they have studied in the college. This is a waste of resources."

engineers that NASSCOM says are Employable. The rest 14 lakhs have each wasted Rs. 10 lakhs of fees. That totals to a staggering sum of around $20 Billion. Over and above this, there is loss of Human Capital. India needs to re-plan the whole Engineering Education system. Government needs to cut down on the number of colleges and improve the quality in the rest.

USA produces around 100,000 (1 Lac) engineers per year for a $16 Trillion economy. India produces 1.5 million (15 lac) Engineers for a $2 Trillion economy. Well, blame it on our huge population.

Required New Skillsets:

a. Conceptual Thinking to make students look beyond books

b. Extended Reality (Memory Studies)

c. Data Analytics, AI, IOT, Robotics, VR & AR

The earlier mass recruiting sector was manufacturing. It used to recruit from the core branches like Electrical, Mechanical, Civil etc. But, Manufacturing is relatively stagnant at 17% of the GDP. So the core branch placements have become very difficult. However, today the market offers plenty of choices for employment, if one looks away from the traditional Engineering and Medical jobs. Hospitality, Retail, Real Estate, Aerospace, Automobile, Media & Entertainment, Graphics & Animation, Fashion, Event Management etc. are the spaces offering tremendous scopes in career building.

The most recent mass recruiter was the IT sector. It grew from scratch to almost 5% of the GDP in a short time. IT employed millions of engineers. Now, IT is also saturating. Only good, skilled IT engineers are in demand.

Today the situation is that most engineers are working in a field that has no connection to what they have studied in the college. This is a waste of resources.

Start-ups are a great leveller today, offering freedom to the Entrepreneurs to innovate and scale business fast, while creating several jobs as well. Entrepreneurship is a boon to the country that solves many problems and benefits all concerned. Of course, this enterprising avenue needs better support ecosystem for growth and sustainability. But, the trend surely is encouraging, creating a silver line in the hovering clouds of anxiety.

GOI (MHRD) Budget for Research:

Government has given impetus to improve and expand research facilities. A grant of Rs. 480Cr for Social Science Research Project under Impactful Policy Research, Rs. 225Cr for research in Basic Sciences, Rs. 1000Cr under Impacting Research, Innovation and Technology (IMPRINT), Rs. 450Cr under Skill Training and Research Institute of Distance Education (STRIDE) to boost research in Humanities, and Rs. 480Cr under Scheme for Promotion of Academic and Research Collaboration (SPARC) for joint research with foreign universities in any discipline has been given by the Ministry.

Conclusion

Considering the not so encouraging scenario with regard to the government's efforts at creating more jobs in the country, hope lies in more entrepreneurial ventures and consideration of less explored avenues by the Indian youth.

A holistic collaboration between the Academics and the Industries offers a Win-Win situation for both and sincere efforts must ensure a mutual support ecosystem in the country. The recently announced skill development program by the Central Government and the State Governments needs sincerity in its implementation but not in isolation of the relevant stakeholders. In the absence of self-regulation in the academic world, the government has to create a supportive yet regulative (not policing) body to ensure quality education, driven solely by the market dynamics. There is no quick-fix solution to this problem, nor will any piecemeal approach suffice. Imparting life skills will enable these young graduates to face challenges and tackle them appropriately with confidence, without losing patience in frustration.

Stephen Hawking said, "The real threat to knowledge is not ignorance but the illusion of knowing."

START-UPS – EMERGING TREND IN INDIA

According to a NASSCOM report, India is one of the fastest growing start-up nations in the world with more than 4,200 start-ups providing over 80,000 jobs. The start-up India programme that was launched by the Government of India with similar support policies by several state governments and industry bodies, have definitely accelerated the growth of start-up culture in India. The growth of the Indian economy can be increased by the better utilisation of resources with new technologies and industries. In 2018, trends shaping the start-up ecosystem in India were consumerism and digital adoption. India's close to 500 Mn internet users and about 350 mn smart phone users, is the biggest market for its acceleration. India has fast-emerged as a start-up nation, attracting international attention and an influx of people investing over the last few years.

"Innovation is lacking in us sorely due to the absence of such an ecosystem in our education and in our society. Research oriented higher education encouraging new ideas could only produce innovative things. No wonder, India lags behind most countries in the world for registering Patents."

Successful Start-ups in India

The infectious trend of start-ups have blossomed several successful business models, some of which have already acquired the status of Unicorns with billion dollars revenues and valuations. OYO Rooms have emerged as the largest hotel room aggregators without owning a single hotel. Flipkart and Big Basket similarly don't own a single retail brand but are the largest retail chains today. Paytm is ubiquitous across India for payments without owning any bank or financial agencies. Food deliveries like Swiggy and Zomato don't own a single restaurant but delivers foods and snacks from a variety of food chains. Nestaway doesn't own a single house but offers houses on rent/lease in several cities today. Netmed doesn't own a single pharmaceutical company but delivers all medicines at the doorstep. There are several such examples of Indian start-ups that are serving their millions of customers online, strengthening the new digital India that has emanated from the burgeoning internet and smartphones. Ideas have created value propositions and established the knowledge economy. India has changed the way it works today. Digital Economy is driving business and lives today, making lives easier for the millions of the consumers.

Today, several start-ups are emerging in most sectors, which is a good sign for the country. Healthcare, Agriculture, Retail, Space, Engineering, Environment, Infrastructure, Power & Energy, Education, Finance, Automobile, Transportation, Art & Craft and even Lifestyle et al have been invaded by a pool of growing young enterprising minds with various automations and solutions. All these have and will ease lives.

The Missing Links

However more often than not, new age business ideas in India today are products of influences. Most Indian start-ups are simple replicas of the successful entities from the developed countries with just local customizations attuning to the Indian market and consumer's need. This won't sustain the success for long and won't make India an economic powerhouse. We cannot continue to be mere copycats. India needs to produce a Microsoft, Google, Facebook, Amazon etc. Innovation is lacking in us sorely due to the absence of such an ecosystem in our education and in our society. Research oriented higher education encouraging new ideas could only produce innovative things. No wonder, India lags behind most countries in the world for registering Patents. Our successful entrepreneurs, industrialists shy away from investing much on R&D and Innovation. Disruptive ideas could only lead to the creation of such wonderful business entities, products and services. In order to bring about a social change and bridge the digital divide, market should be rural focused, mobile centric, socially relevant. Social Entrepreneurship would be able to address the challenges that India has been facing.

Encouraging a culture of entrepreneurship in educational institutions

Entrepreneurial Education will lead to development and offering holistic, scalable social solutions. There have been talks on building a robust entrepreneurship ecosystem in India, and we are the third largest such technology start-ups community in the world. However, we are ranked 68 in Global Innovation Index by GEDI, just above Panama and just below Kazakhstan. Similarly, in the Global Innovation Index, India is ranked 60. Interestingly, Switzerland, USA, and the UK are top-ranked in both these indices. Many of our social issues (eg: potable water for all, waste management, environment) are still unsolved or partially solved.

Entrepreneurship is vital for stimulating economic growth, employment opportunities and social well-being in all societies. This is particularly true in the developing world, where successful small businesses are the primary engines of job creation and poverty reduction. India should strive towards an Innovation-driven economy.

Education needs overhaul. It is not just about establishing an entrepreneurship lab but to incorporate the principles of entrepreneurship and innovation in every subject being taught. Additionally, emphasis should also be laid on developing student's skills of dialogue and clear and fluent communication (both general and business). Teaching should move towards collaborative and experiential learning, introducing creativity and innovative skills. This is possible through project based learning and by making a strong connection with the society and the industry. Innovation and social responsibility when interwoven in the curriculum of all disciplines and culture of entrepreneurship when encouraged, students enjoy the freedom and would be tempted to try out.

Customer-led innovations will create customer delight and more businesses. The informal entrepreneurs could assemble and interact with the end-users and customers to design and produce their products and services as required and preferred by them.

"Social Entrepreneurship with support and encouragement from the beginning with innovative ideas and solutions, could address our numerous challenges in various aspects of our daily lives and living."

Global Entrepreneurship Monitor defines entrepreneurs based on whether their start was either due to a necessity or an opportunity. People start opportunity based ventures because they spot requirement around them. India has large number of necessity-based entrepreneurship and a few opportunity-based entrepreneurships. We need more of the latter to create wealth and jobs. Efforts must be made making the students learn and understand all about Entrepreneurship through the Case Studies and methods. Several premier B-Schools in India have started core courses in the first year of MBA on Entrepreneurial Mind-set and the concept of entrepreneurship inside the companies. This follows a course on the Action oriented entrepreneurship, educating the students learn developing a venture.

Several colleges in India have set up Incubators to shape up dreams of the students with adventurous minds. The main purpose of an incubator is to help entrepreneurs in setting up and running their businesses. Besides, infrastructural support, the students also get mentoring by the professors and at times from the visiting representatives from the industry.

Accelerators are enablers for start-ups not just in terms of the business educational aspect but also to introduce them to the right network for mentorship, funding and future growth. Domain specific start-up accelerator helps the start-ups quicken their go-to-market strategy. Team, Idea and faster Growth Rate get evaluated for investment.

Knowledge Economy: New Age Economy

Technology operates as a very important cog in the wheels of progress and development. Businesses driven with technology create knowledge economy and countries around the world rule the roost when follow this. The academia, Indian Inc and the Government must acknowledge the power of entrepreneurship and make combined efforts to encourage this among the students and the youth, which in turn would help them all and the country would progress rapidly towards economic empowerment, wealth creation and employability.

The enterprising young persons with their entrepreneurship ventures and with success have surely impacted the society and several bright young minds have followed suit to ideate and give wings to their dreams assiduously. And this surely will spur other such enterprising minds from across India to venture into the same, creating value propositions and employment opportunities as well. Social Entrepreneurship with support and encouragement from the beginning with innovative ideas and solutions, could address our numerous challenges in various aspects of our daily lives and living. Remember, many of them have succeeded in their efforts without any support ecosystem...perhaps even with no encouragement or support from either the government, district administration or any trade

& industry bodies. Identifying and nurturing the innovative ideas, helping in designing the business models with necessary seed capitals to formulate and go to the market, offering a business support ecosystem and incubation facilities would surely help the start-up industry in growing and moving in the right direction to help Indian economy improve substantially.

LESSONS FROM FAILURE

─────◦◉◦─────

Success introduces you to the world but failure introduces the world to you. Nothing could be truer than this. You have been listening to the success stories of the accomplished people but you are unable to reach their heights. Now, listen to the failures to learn and understand what not to do/ commit which the success stories will never tell or teach. There is always struggle and pain under the glossy surface. Success covers them up or glorifies, as it suits the chosen narrative, but failure magnifies the underbelly and more often than not, become the raison d'être. The Sun Temple- *Konark was not built in a day.*

Like Success, Failure could also happen anywhere- in our Relationships, in Business, in the Job & Career, in Studies & Education, in Sports & Games, in Social Works, in Politics, in Research, in Projects, in War, in Personal & Professional lives. What causes them? Can they be mitigated, if not stopped completely? Although, there is no magic-pill for cure but a complete analysis of the Cause-Effect scenario would surely throw lights into this syndrome

> *There is always struggle and pain under the glossy surface. Success covers them up or glorifies, as it suits the chosen narrative, but failure magnifies the underbelly and more often than not, become the raison d'être.*

that afflicts us all at some time or the other and learning from this sincerely, we could attempt at the mitigation. Error is the backyard of perfection.

It is also said that success is 99% perspiration and 1% luck hence the planning, efforts and the execution are very much important in their outcome. We may not have complete control over the external factors that could have a bearing on the results, but our house should be in order and we should do our home-works thoughtfully and act smartly, considering all aspects concerned.

Nothing succeeds like success. You will be looked down upon, criticised, trolled and even may get abused for being a failure but all that changes when you achieve success. Ugly looks beautiful, all that's bad looks good, wrongs become right or at least the response could be a weak murmur at best if on disagreement, so on & so forth. This is the irony of this world, which only loves and respects success and failure remains lonely. "Success has many fathers, failure is an orphan."

Let's talk about Business and Entrepreneurship, may be in the start-up context or similar such new businesses. What goes wrong that certain people and certain businesses fail and fold up faster? Dreams shatter, losses incurred, hurt and dejected. When looked back and on the hindsight, several issues crop up and an honest and objective analysis would bring about facts that were the reasons of failure. Let's do a post-mortem, dissecting the issues leading to the business loss and subsequent closure.

KPMG Report on Start-up Valuation in 2020 finds out five primary reasons for the fallouts in Indian context:

1. Lack of Market Needs – 42%

2. Cash Exhaustion – 29%

3. Lack of Right Team/Founders Discord – 23%

4. Competition – 19%

5. Weak Business Model & Lack of Marketing – 14%

Let me elaborate on each of the key issues that need proper attention to avoid any pitfalls and discord, leading to possible subsequent failure. All these details, as explained here, are borne mostly out of my personal experiences as the failed start-up entrepreneur and also as is being observed now in my current role as start-up mentor and business advisor, in this space mostly. Perhaps, I am being sought more today as a business advisor to the larger companies and as a mentor to several start-ups across India, because failure has given me more clarity and I'm able use my thought leadership better, being able to relate to them and guide them correctly. Observing their faster growth and early success, under my guidance, is not just gratifying as their mentor/advisor, but also reiterates my conviction and leadership, which were being questioned earlier.

A. The Idea/Product & The Market

It's 5% idea and 95% execution.

Ideas should be market driven and not imposed on it. Once you have identified the clear gap between the demand and the supply and a strong need for something, ideation could help. Often, fascinated by own idea, people try to force a market-fit which eventually falters. Ideas could be good so long as it addresses the gap in the market, fulfilling the growing need of large prospective consumers, who are willing to pay for it.

Validate your ideas repeatedly through the experts and knowledgeable professionals to refine the same and make not just market ready but sustainable as well, stitching together the loose ends and making it robust and as much fool-proof as possible. Idea should identify the gap between the demand and supply in the relevant domain that is genuinely needed in the market. More importantly, it should have people paying for it and that will be crucial. Market-fit is important hence, ideas should be market driven and aligned. Problem occurs when the venture gets driven by our ideas that we get obsessed with, but the market is either non-existent or not fertile enough or ready yet to accept that. You will falter in your way sooner than the later.

Ideas also should remain flexible to change course later, if so desired or if the market demands. We tend to get narcissistic and obsessed with our own ideas hence, stay rigid and resist to change, ignoring the market dynamics.

> *We tend to get narcissistic and obsessed with our own ideas hence, stay rigid and resist to change, ignoring the market dynamics.*

It is always important to ensure that the intended buyers and beneficiaries would be willing to pay for using your ideas, solutions and products. Ideally, a market survey prior to venturing into the chosen business, helps understanding the market fully and hence, could position it appropriately.

There are even possibilities that your idea, product or solution aren't entirely new and exist elsewhere if not in the same market. If persisted with, it's better to tweak the same, conducive to that market and hence, localize it, in line with the prevailing market characteristics and prevailing consumer behaviour. Once, penetrated into it fully and got the foothold, you may gradually bring in your original ideas to have the control of the target market to rule over, though sustainability hinges on your vision, long-term plans and business acumen.

Rather than casting a huge national or global net trying to encompass anyone and everyone, niche websites allow you to focus your energies on one particular market and subject and do it well!

- Start out small – walk before you run and allow yourself to make your mistakes when you're small so that you can get organized for success as you eventually grow

- Focus on a smaller market that will give you more precise targeting options and better chances to achieve greater ROI on your investments

- Create important partnerships early on that will create more opportunities down the road

B. Partner/Co-Founder

It's important for a Start-up Founder to evaluate the Products/Solution with regard to the target market and if the energy, calibre and mind set of peers joining it match yours. Mere being friends or knowing each other socially wouldn't help. The test begins when the going gets tough and challenges surmount beyond control. It's a well-documented fact that partnerships fail often and businesses crumble with the infighting between the Co-Founders, for various reasons. Founder's discord is attributed to about 23% of start-up business failure reasons, as per a recent KPMG report.

In a coalition government, we have noticed that the parties coming together draft a collectively agreed Common Minimum Program (CMP) to form that as their binding factor. Straying from this creates discord and squabble. This merely underlines the importance of adjustment in any relationship, but only if we value the same and continue to respect each other, having mutual trust as well.

Hence, it's most important to have a written Founder's Agreement or Director's Agreement note, duly signed and if possible even notarised, clearly defining roles and responsibilities divided between. One Founder focuses on Fund Raising while the rest stay focused and work on respective roles but together. Put your Egos aside. Fundraising sucks. It is more fun to keep the company progressing than to get turned down each day. Money won't solve all problems in the company always. It's the resolve to stay together and support each other in times of difficulties, that keeps the flock together and even two opposite personalities breathing alike.

From my observations as a Start-up Mentor and as an Entrepreneur, there are several friction points, and in my opinion 60 to 70 percent start-ups fail because the Founders couldn't stick together and aligned with their vision and squabbled with role plays, nursing aspirations during the progress, mired with their egos and mutual mistrust.

The test begins when the going gets tough and challenges surmount beyond control. It's a well-documented fact that partnerships fail often and businesses crumble with the infighting between the Co-Founders, for various reasons. Founder's discord is attributed to about 23% of start-up business failure reasons

A founders' agreement is a legally binding contract, usually in writing, that outlines the roles, rights, and responsibilities of each owner in a business. It could be a standalone document, or it could be incorporated into corporate bylaws, an LLC operating agreement, or partnership agreement. It is designed to protect each founder's interests and to prevent conflict down the line.

Here are some of the reasons why having a founders' agreement is essential:

- Clarifies each owner's role in the business
- Provides a structure for resolving disputes among founders
- Provides clarity if and when a partner wants to enter or exit the business
- Protects minority owners
- Signals to investors that you have a serious business

Include the following in the Co-Founder's Agreement Document:

a. Each Co-Founder's roles and responsibilities

b. Equity Breakdowns

c. Intellectual Property

d. Salary and Compensation

e. Exit Clauses

f. Contractual Communications and Dispute Resolution

Visiting and consulting with the corporate lawyer helps drafting the same to make it a legal document but only after the co-founders sign on it within a timeframe, after reviewing it considerably and having the hard talking, in between.

C. Bootstrap

Every business needs a minimum amount of required money to start with. We cannot think of starting our business only with our ideas and using other's money. Well, you might as well do that though, couldn't be an ideal situation in the long run for various reasons and possible push and pulls. Ideally, a minimum of one year and a maximum of two years money should be kept in hand to operate without external borrowings. Optimum utilization of minimum resources and 'cutting the coat according to the clothes' help managing business affairs and daily operations. Flamboyancy and over indulgence should be avoided at all costs at the beginning, at least till decent traction happens and revenue generated regularly.

What do Microsoft, Apple, HP and Amazon have in common? All four of them began in the garages of their founders. Silicon Valley is full of stories of technology giants with such humble beginnings. Facebook's Mark Zuckerberg first set out to turn his dorm room project into a lasting business. And near home, Infosys had started from a garage and Flipkart from a small 2-BHK rented apartment.

> *Optimum utilization of minimum resources and 'cutting the coat according to the clothes' help managing business affairs and daily operations.*

We have heard several stories of successful businesses of how start-ups had initially started in garages under bootstrap mode and that should continue to be the role models for the others, venturing out with their exciting ideas, solutions and products. It's prudent to maintain and follow fiscal discipline at every step of the entrepreneurial journey, without succumbing to the temptation of showmanship and flamboyancy. It helps maintaining a low profile with cost control. It's better always to avoid as much to have a fancy office space, spending unnecessarily in huge rent, doing up the interiors and blocking precious money in the large security deposits and purchasing gadgets to flaunt. These are considered avoidable luxuries which could lighten the small purse considerably, thereby putting unnecessary pressure on the pockets that could result in restricting your operation considerably.

- Cost control is the practice of identifying and reducing business expenses to increase profits, and it starts with the budgeting process.

- Cost control is an important factor in maintaining and growing profitability.

- Outsourcing is a common method to control costs because many businesses find it cheaper to pay a third party to perform a task than to take on the work within the company.

  Controlling costs is one way to plan for a target net income, which is computed using the following formula:

  Sales - fixed costs - variable costs = target **net income**

A minimum of three years to five years' budget and business plan helps in not just controlled planning but it's financial prudent to have such clarity at the beginning which should be reviewed periodically to follow on the expenses while striving to enhance income.

D. Business Model & Plan

Every business idea, in order to succeed in the target market must devise a suitable business model with strategies and thoughtful plans. The same needs to be well documented with relevant supportive inputs in spread-sheets, excel sheets and in PPT formats. It is necessary for you to communicate your ideas and the devised business models to your target audience for clarity and conviction, influencing them in your favour, inducing to pay for using them. Ultimate aim is to have customers and earning revenues, which are the necessary oxygen for breathing and survival. But, in this crowded market with competitions all along and attention deficit by the people in general in this world of information overload, one has to identify its USP to differentiate and sustain. Therefore, besides the customary metrics and relevant figures, your narrative must project a stronger storyline that attracts the undivided attention in the market, helping you earning your revenue and continue the business flow, unhindered. And this differentiating factor has to be identified both in your ideas and the business model. Ideas need to be monetised. However, flexibility and alternate options need to be kept ready always to address any eventuality and in the changed market dynamics.

There have been several instances of good businesses folding up prematurely. On closer examination, we get to know these factors influencing their fate as far as the business model is concerned:

1.   Ideas imposed upon the non-existent market

2.   Run-of-the-mill ideas or cloning existing ones

3.   Unable to keep pace with the changing market dynamics and changing demands, in the absence of a Plan-B ready

At times, the founders get obsessed with their ideas and stay rigid even in the face of market resistances or when the market dynamics change. Unless in tune with the market demands, your business model will falter mid-way, hence keeping pace with the changing times, help sustain in the long run. A perceived shortcoming could be overcome with harder push and more efforts but that even doesn't guarantee success. Thus, the differentiating factors need to be brought out clearly in the open and communicated well to the market, with persistence and dedication, but more with smart thinking and acts.

E. Traction

Your venture will succeed only when you will be able to get your target audience paying you for your solutions, products and services. Revenue generation and making profits are the key drivers. Hence, your efforts and focus should aim to elicit this result at the earliest. When you start earning, your confidence soars, your business grows and investors appreciate.

> *When you start earning, your confidence soars, your business grows and investors appreciate.*

Traction relies on your go-to-market strategy and marketing efforts, but only when you are able to get your offers related to and connected with the target market, inducing the target audiences to accept and purchase. So, revenue generation should be your immediate and primary concern and focus. Hence, it's imperative to understand what triggers traction and what sustains it along the way.

F. Funding & Investor's Deck

Start-ups frequently prepare a "pitch deck" to present their company to prospective angel or venture capital investors. The pitch deck typically consists of not more than a minimum of five to a maximum of ten slides in a Power Point (PPT) presentation, intended to showcase the company's products, technology, team to the investors and the reason for seeking the required funding.

Ideally, the Investors Pitch Deck should follow the following and shouldn't take more than 10 minutes maximum to present to the investors present.

Slide1: 3-4 liner summery

Slide2: Pain Point, market gaps

Slide3: Solution on offer to address the pains

Slide4: Traction & Clients

Slide5: Core Team

Slide6: Funding request & Equity offer: Why?-How Much?-What For?

For back-up, spread-sheets and excel sheets should be kept ready in detail, especially elaborating on the financials, the minimum three years'

Balance Sheet and Projections and a clear Roadmap. This should be shared with the investment prospects, which show interest and wishes to carry out further dialogue with you.

Broadly, in my opinion, your Business Idea should have these considered well, possibly packed into 6 slides max:

a. What's the PROBLEM that you are trying to address and solve?

b. What's your SOLUTION to the Problem?

c. USP - what's Unique and Novel about your Solution?

d. COMPETITION & BARRIER TO ENTRY - how easy it is to replicate your solution?

e. REVENUE MODEL - how will you make money off your solution? Make a minimum of 3 years Business Plan and Balance Sheet - Cash Inflow and Outflow details

f. TARGET MARKET - Size of your Market and what Percentage of it you will be targeting to achieve in what time frame? Profile your Customer.

> *There are two major drivers that matter to raise money successfully:*
>
> *1. Your Team*
>
> *2. Your Idea is Interesting to them.*
>
> *Focus on your cash flow first.*

g. YOUR PRODUCT & SERVICE - how will this Add Value

h. MILESTONES - Prototypes, Patents, Pilots.....1-2-3 year's Road map

i. FUNDING - Why & how much money is required and how will you be spending them, to achieve what?

j. THE TEAM

Remember, the primary objective of the Investors is to:

a. Know You all in the Core Team, understanding about your Capabilities & Team Spirit

b. See your Clarity of Thoughts & Confidence to Drive Business

c. Clear Long-term Plans

d. Technology Integration and Improvement

Hence, your Pitch-deck slides should only reflect on these themes to create strong interest and further curiosity at the first meeting. Never try to close the deal in this meeting. It will be considered positive only when the Investors ask you for a second meeting soon. In fact, the first three slides are the deciding factors hence; your pitch should care for this. It's a gross error to pack in too much information with too many slides. That's overkilling.

There are two major drivers that matter to raise money successfully: 1. Your Team 2. Your Idea is Interesting to them. Of course, incredible growth rate would easily attract the Investors, but that's not always the case with all start-ups and not necessary either. Valuation should not be the measuring stick of your success. Focus on Cash Flow first.

Fund raising is a critical driver in progress but not many business leaders possess this ability. Ironically at times, this becomes Achilles' heel for the leadership and many a times, failing the venture to succeed. If possible, team should consider hiring an experienced finance professional, having the experience of raising funding for start-ups.

G. Strategy (of Product & Business)

Your idea/product/solutions are good but that doesn't ensure success. You can have the best of products but if not marketed well and positioned in the market properly with necessary PR and Branding, it may not sustain long, especially in the face of competition and a less loyal customer. Market is too crowded and customers are pampered with choices hence, visibility and brand recall are equally important and necessary.

Business strategy is very important. This calls for complete understanding of your product/solutions/services and also that of the target market in general, and for your offers especially.

But most important is product positioning and branding. Let's take the classic case of the Tata Nano, the revolutionary people's car that created huge buzz across the world and was just rightly priced to suit the smaller pockets of the target market, the middle-class Indians, dreaming of graduating from the 2-wheelers to a 4-wheeler, notwithstanding the no-frill option. After all, a car is a car for such a person, no matter what size and facilities it may offer. The automobile world was amused yet excited and the initial responses were akin to the opening of a super star's blockbuster. But, where is Nano today? Why did it fail abruptly, belying all plans and support? If we put aside the other reasons like the technical issues, production delays and the likes, which were true, but the issue that stood out tall and needs sincere consideration is

- Product Positioning – the Omissions & Commissions

The automaker was under the misconception that the low price would be enough to motivate people to buy the Nano. They did not account for their positioning it as a cheap vehicle which, in India's markets, translates to low quality. So, bad marketing strategy was perhaps the key reason for the Tata Nano's failure. Market perception was ignored which finally derailed it.

The Tata Nano failed to be the innovative car it was aspired to be and is still considered one of the biggest tragedies in the history of the Indian Automotive Industry.

H. Marketing, PR & Branding

Having a product isn't just about your latest launch or achievement plan, it's about delivering a message to the world about what you've accomplished or planning to do. Any product, popular or not, doesn't guarantee success, on its own. It has to be worked on. With media reaching from print to web and mobile, there's no time like the present to show your-self off to the public. Well calibrated publicity is the key to the success and popularity of anything that needs to be consumed by the public, especially when the market is crowded with several similar ones, the efforts need to be that much more and different.

> *Well calibrated publicity is the key to the success and popularity of anything that needs to be consumed by the public, especially when the market is crowded with several similar ones, the efforts need to be that much more and different.*

Every Business has three distinct parts integral and important to it. They are: Marketing, Business Development and Sales, of course the all-important product itself. The latter (Sales) being the bottom-line in all businesses, is helped and aided by the former two (BD & Marketing). In order to achieve Sales, you have to Develop Business (planning, need creation, developing, nurturing and bringing everything under control) and engage in Marketing (PR, Branding & Advertisement for awareness, visibility, acceptability & popularity).

Visibility is required in personal as well as professional lives. Either an individual or an organization needs to communicate with their target market in particular and to the world in general. Reaching out to them and establishing relationship with them for mutual benefit and attracting their attention to you requires thoughtful planning, handled professionally. Public Relation (PR) and Branding are very much essential towards these and targeted communication would benefit. When this aspect of a product, an organization or a talent is/are handled professionally and created a positive and a strong image in the concerned market, the improved visibility and image help in impacting activities and businesses positively. Talent speaks but projection by others help. It really feels awkward to tom-tom about self. Professional support is desired by the professional, who understands business and is effective in connecting them to their markets.

This exercise demands high quality professionalism and persistent efforts to build up the product gradually, successfully.

People often think that marketing is all about the current buzz word-Digital Marketing. But it's not just that but much more and much beyond. And it's a continuous process. It's erroneous to think that, mere digital marketing would elicit the desired results. This is merely exhibiting your ignorance and underestimating the powers and potentials of marketing, which is a vast canvas. Right use of the selective tools of the same, as relevant, would help. Problem occurs when the entrepreneurs, especially from a pure technology background, give less importance to marketing and branding, thinking that their product alone with little bit of marketing push, would drive business. Of course, good product helps in the business sustainability. But not without strong marketing push. And please remember that marketing doesn't mean advertising alone, but staying engaged with the target audience and touching their heart, pushing for addressing the need, and at times even help creating one. Several instances are there in the market to prove this point.

A word of caution: excess of everything is bad. Going overboard kills the business, evoking all kinds of undesired negative emotions. So, it is pertinent to draw the line somewhere, a boundary not to be breached.

Conclusion

It's not being utopian nor speaking perfection but ideally, one needs to have as much of these to avoid possible pitfalls, leading to failures.

a. Have everything written down clearly in black & white before starting the venture and document them properly. Spell out your *Magnacarta* and follow them sincerely, in letter and spirit, having right check & balances in place.

b. Being unable to have control over your activities and overly depending on others, becomes your weak point, inviting trouble in the long run. Try to be on top of your assigned job.

c. Men are complex creatures and wired to take control mostly. This often triggers conflicts, leading to possible showdowns and breaking down in relationships. Mutual respect is a must and disagreements need to be professionally addressed with dignity and without emotions. However respecting mutual sentiments and feelings is appreciated.

d. No man is perfect. Instead of magnifying one's weaknesses and shortcomings, it's better to utilise each other's strengths, ignoring the negatives. In order to maintain the Team Spirit and healthy Camaraderie, synergies should be established, complementing each other's strengths. Inter-personal relationship is very important for a healthy work atmosphere and peaceful workplace. It's about relationship management with mutual respect.

e. Remember, it's always a Team work and working in tandem, supporting each other, leveraging on one's strengths and with a passion to succeed together while walking hand-in-hand in the journey, ensure success and peace.

f. Focus should be on traction and early revenue generation. Cash inflow is a strong booster ingredient and your entrepreneurial journey hinges on it.

g. Relating to the investor community is an Art and Science. Your appropriate communication and strong business projection, laced with dollops of leadership confidence, get their attention, inducing them to put their money on you.

h. "Procrastination is the thief of time." "A stitch in time saves nine." It helps being in action, rather than being a day-dreamer or stay put relying on fate.

i. Your idea should be market driven, not sitting obsessed with it and holding onto even when the wheels start wobbling and stop moving. Flexibility in strategy and having a Plan-B ready in place helps moving over and staying afloat.

j.   Failure is the pillar of success. When one door shuts, more open. We just have to work harder with perseverance and determination, without giving up in the face of challenges or when tripped over. Get up and walk on. Find your purpose. Listen to your calls. Failure is just a comma; it's not the end of your journey. Look around you... people with much more pains, lot more losses, are still smiling and moved on with success, later on...rediscovering ideas and reinventing themselves.

As an entrepreneur, I have learnt these the hard way. Hence, am sharing with you the same for your benefit and success, so that you won't trip over and fall half-way. Perhaps, I have become more successful and in greater demand today as a Start-up Mentor and Business Advisor to companies because of these lessons learnt and humble understandings from my own failures and shortcomings. It's gratifying to see and I take pride in saying that my contributions and value additions are being publicly acknowledged and appreciated by most of the start-ups I've been mentoring and the companies I'm associated with in their advisory boards. Emboldened by this turnaround, I am even ready today to take the steering wheel to drive businesses as the Captain of the ship, if so proposed.

Life is the biggest Teacher and learners always improve.

What if I fail?

Oh my darling, what if you fly?

MAKE IN INDIA: FOCUS ON SOCIAL SECURITY & INTERNAL SECURITY

India is a vast country with abundance of rich flora, fauna, minerals and human resources comprising today mostly of young Indians. The democratic dividends need to be effectively utilized and honed with for its overall development and inclusiveness. Make in India is a step in the right direction towards making India self-reliant and developed. Our Hon'ble Prime Minister has rightly emphasized on this and I join a billion people to congratulate him for the same. It's a laudable effort and all Indians must come forward to contribute their mite for its success.

Manufacturing and producing everything possible in India would not only benefit its citizens but will make India a truly developed economic powerhouse. It has the potential and resources available only sincere efforts and a changed mindset would take the country a long way. India has vast educated, English speaking and skilled people. Industries would benefit immensely with their availability.

"India spends 1.4 percent of its GDP on social protection, among the lowest in Asia, far lower than China, Sri Lanka, Thailand, and even Nepal."

Making in India will boost production, increase employment, enhance the economy, improve the living standards as well as bring prices down of various commodities while reducing dependency on imports thereby saving precious revenues and money.

Green energy may renew job hopes and has the potential to create about 3 lakh jobs in 5 years. Apart from giving the country cleaner environment, a study has forecast. Wind power, ground mounted solar projects and rooftop solar projects are the ones need to be invested in and encourage with. Besides sizeable employment, it creates entrepreneurs too. The latter are not only producers of solutions and services through technology but also help in generating employment. Entrepreneurship must be encouraged wholeheartedly.

Emphasis should also be given on the improvement and development of skillsets of the citizens through Skill India program.

Social Security

The Republic of India guarantees several measures towards the social security of its citizens. In an economic revolution, advent of social security will balance the growth and maintain social and economic parity. This is very much desired for any progressive country. Make in India may be the answer to India's unemployment puzzle. Overall, job scenario today is not in a happy state and indicates dire situation. Unless sincere and planned focus is trained on this issue, this may lead to social strife.

Social security and Welfare should be accorded maximum focus. India still does not have a minimum social security system for its citizens. This is worrisome and cries for urgent attention of the policy makers and the administration.

"Waiving off loans won't help but improvement in the agriculture mechanism through scientific approach using technology and internet would aid the workers and farmers. Thoughtful use of Remote Sensing through Satellites and use of Geographic Information Systems (GIS) with Data Analytics would surely help in forecasting and assessing situations."

India spends 1.4 percent of its GDP on social protection, among the lowest in Asia, far lower than China, Sri Lanka, Thailand, and even Nepal.

Two aspects of social security – Protection and Promotion....protection against fall in living standards and living conditions and enhanced living conditions, helping everyone overcome persistent capabilities deprivation for a universal social security.

India's growth story of the last two decades has had one recurring theme: that the pattern of economic growth is accentuating insecurities. Yet, there continues to be a deep divide over whether the gains from growth ought to be ploughed back to achieve social security for everyone. Social security has come to be linked to job benefits, tying it to one's status as a worker in the formal or the informal economy when, fundamentally, it originates from the notion of ensuring everyone protection against vulnerability and deprivation.

Social security is needed for the young unemployed, employed, elderly persons, women and children in jobs, income, healthcare, education and sanitation. Successive governments have been introducing and running various social welfare schemes but has not benefited the citizens as yet. Aadhar is surely a great unifying tool to offer single national identity as well as linking up all these schemes to truly benefit the citizens, eliminating middlemen while making the distribution process simpler and transparent. Waiving off loans won't help but improvement in the agriculture mechanism through scientific approach using technology and internet would aid the workers and farmers. Thoughtful use of Remote Sensing through Satellites and use of Geographic Information Systems (GIS) with Data Analytics would surely help in forecasting and assessing situations.

Government also should plan for the support social mechanism for the older people. Quality Old Age Homes with all comforts and facilities would give them dignity and self-respect. Similarly, social support and security mechanisms for the girls and women with nutrition and vaccination plans for the children would create a healthy and equitable society. Pension schemes and Medical Support are twin support tools that are a must to support and help the citizens.

India's soft power needs to be harnessed on at the global stage. Yoga has been accorded its legitimate position under the sun and I congratulate our Modi government for making this an annual International event. India's rich wellness alternate therapies like Ayurveda would offer the global citizens a holistic life and peaceful living.

Internal Security

Given the complex and varied nature of threats, India requires a comprehensive internal security strategy involving five components: Political, Military, Social, Economic and Diplomatic. Apart from the physical aggression changes in this global world, the all-pervasive internet and digital technology pose a graver challenge today. Digital and cyber security aspects need thoughtful attention and required mechanism needs to be developed to protect the economy and the business.

The left wing internal security threats, social strife, communalism and global terrorism are the challenges that India has been grappling with for long. These issues are crippling normal lives as well as disturbing business and social harmony.

Make in India lion has to stride along the social and economic paths for a balanced and equitable society with inclusive growth and gender equation. Social and family value systems cannot be ignored further that India has followed with.

Medical Tourism

Today India has emerged as a preferred destination for medical tourism in tertiary treatment. World class medical infrastructure, world's best healthcare experts, inexpensive treatment with wellness centers for holistic treatment besides exotic tourist destinations come as a complete package for the discerning global health travellers. With a focused sanitation and hygiene program, health conscious international citizens would prefer to visit India over other destinations. Government should support and promote this to the world in a planned and systematic manner. It has a twin potential of increasing forex as well as generating employment. In order to make this healthcare industry more homogenous and structured, government must introduce a regulatory mechanism soon. This will not only regulate the unorganized healthcare sector but would bring down costs substantially eliminating the middlemen and the unsavory nexus prevalent today. Digital India and online transactions would help matters improve making the experience hassle free for the patients. Subsidies could be offered to set up quality medical facilities in smaller towns aiding the remote regions with Telemedicine and Tele-radiology. India could offer these services to the underdeveloped countries in the world and with exchange of knowledge, could enhance the skillsets of the Doctors in these countries.

Today there are over 5 crore unemployed people in the country. Through healthcare workers training on medical technology can contribute to employment generation. There are about 65 lakh vacancies in the allied health sector today.

India's Soft Power

India's rich tradition and knowledge could be the answer to the global woes. Let's join hands to promote them and introduce to the global citizens with pride.

Yoga and India's traditional wellness centers with Ayurvedic treatment and Naturopathy are the twin Indian elements that we could sell to the world to keep everyone healthy and in peace without being medicated and with dangerous side effects. Chinese people still follow their traditional medicines and exercise regimes with martial arts coexisting with advanced technology. India has all these of its own that it could aggressively sell to the world. Wellness Cafes catering to the contemporary taste and pallet would be a great idea that could be encouraged and patronized with immense commercial viability.

India has great classical dance forms like Odissi, Bharatnatyam, Kuchipudi, Kathakalli, Mohiniattam, Kathak etc. Since ages, individual artists are touring around the world teaching students their dances while performing in these countries to an awestruck and admiring international audience. Government of India could set up International Cultural Centers in various countries in a collaborative effort to allow these talented artists to perform, train and earn as well. Exchange of artists and cultural troupes would foster global brotherhood.

Conclusion

Make in India would help the country in branding itself better and expanding the market across the world for all Indians while improving exports and earning more revenues besides respect.

India has to be selective in its production since no country consumes all that it produces. We must ask ourselves and be clear about, do we want Exports, Cost Reduction or Employment Generation? The Make in India has to be nuanced accordingly.

Make in India program while promoting self-reliance, should focus on Social Security, Internal Security while selling its Soft Power for better Branding and global leadership for a balanced act.

Advantage India.

DISRUPTIVE INNOVATION: TECHNOLOGY & BUSINESS

Dreaming is an essential part of creative thinking. A dreamer is an achiever as long as she/he follows it up with meticulous plan with determination, and similarly an entrepreneur lives in the future while working thoughtfully on the present. Essential attributes required are:

- Domain Knowledge

- Learning Appetite

- Problem Solving

With innovative ideas and disruptive solutions, if communicated to the target audience and to the chosen market appropriately, it will bring in the desired results. Clarity of thoughts coupled with confidence will propel the ideas faster in the desired direction. When the consumer is willing to pay for it, customer traction entails. When the same is scaled up gradually, keeping up with the times, business soars rapidly and success endures.

Welcome to the future of business where technology plays a key role, aiding the innovative ideas and disruptive solutions of the entrepreneurs. New age technologies like Artificial Learning (AI), Machine Learning (ML), Internet of Things (IoT), Block Chain, Augmented Reality and Virtual Reality

(AR & VR), Robotics, Drones and UAVs have made all aspects of life and business, futuristic and fairy-tale like, remarkably reducing the human presence and engagement, computing in a lightning speed, managing several terabytes of data, simultaneously.

In the world of medicine, AI and the Doctors will work side by side to take care of the patient's health. For example, AI can now warn GPs that their patients are at risk of developing severe kidney damage up to two days early, with the potential to save hundreds of thousands of lives every year.

The machine learning model has been developed jointly by DeepMind Health, a division of Google, and the US Department of Veterans Affairs (VA), a federal agency that provides healthcare services to military veterans across the US.

Here in India, Clinical Data Management with organizations like the Centre for Cellular and Molecular Platforms (C-Comp) and National Centre for Biological Sciences (NCBS) besides several Integrated DNA based labs/clinics for personalised medicines and personal diagnostics, have helped the healthcare and medical sectors in improving their works considerably, thereby benefiting the patients the world over.

Molecular diagnostics has revolutionised Oncology treatment.

- Molecular Tumour Analysis
- Target Treatment
- Precision Medicine

In Cancer research, Oncogenomics helps in improving Diagnosis, Prognosis and Therapeutics.

Healthcare is one of the most promising areas likely to be transformed by machine learning systems, which are able to sift through large amounts of data quickly and find meaningful patterns.

AI is already being tested as a way to more quickly diagnose everything from breast cancer to diabetic retinopathy, even in Ayurveda for dealing with athlete's injuries, and has been found to be significantly more accurate and speedy than human experts, allowing doctors to treat patients before they deteriorate.

Voice based Robotic applications like Alexa, many traditional activities can be customised to tailor make the day to day needs in the old age or for the senior citizen/elderlies/aged, suiting their needs and requirements.

Legacy software versus Proprietary software and Cloud Computing (SAAS)

Decades ago software was designed and developed with older languages like Fortran, Cobol, that still continue to be used by several organizations the world over, who still have not migrated to the prevailing new proprietary languages and the open source, due to either in fear of huge changes in the records and archives or just being resistant to change. It is not just the cost factor but the ease of doing business, get impacted and improve. Today, large data volume needs to be crunched faster, integrating seamlessly with other applications even on different platforms, on the fly.

Digital disruptions are eating up the traditional businesses each passing day. Travel agents and their agencies have become obsolete and defunct in 2019 as online portals have become handy and popular. It's like the gradual disappearance of the ubiquitous photo studios, dotting the city landscape with the advent of mobile phones with quality cameras on them.

Did global tour and travel chains like Thomas Cook, Sita Travels ever had dreamt of becoming obsolete and defunct, unsustainable one day, what with their swanky and plush front offices in city upscale? Availability of inexpensive alternative options empowering decision making process directly without external involvement popularised online businesses the world over. Why are the iconic companies closing down and what the Start-ups should be mindful of. Home grown travel and ticketing portals like Make My Trip and Go Ibibo etc are the popular and automatic choices of millions today.

Companies and businesses that can innovate adapt and adopt technology faster and understand the market dynamics would only sustain and survive though, not without jostling for space in the market with several clones around, undercutting each other on price discounts.

The emergence of "Third Business Model" if permitted to say so, through the popular e-commerce portals like Amazon, Alibaba and Air Bnb have revolutionized today's businesses and consumption pattern. These aggregators serve as e-platforms, extending their business ecosystem through third party companies. Such business models are less resource intensive and need less investment as well. In India, Flipkart, OYO, Nestaway and the likes have established themselves successfully, following the same business model. Offline businesses are finding it difficult to compete with their On-line counterparts and voices of dissent have been on the ascendancy. In this Platform Business Model, the E-Tailer provides a platform for both producers and consumers to exchange their resources.

Number of Artificial Intelligence (AI) acquisitions since 2010:

Apple: 20 acquisitions

Google: 14 acquisitions

Microsoft: 10 acquisitions

Facebook: 08 acquisitions

Intel: 08 acquisitions

Amazon: 05 acquisitions

A peek into the business leadership and the prevalent market dynamics would present an interesting insight into the intricacies of businesses and the leadership psyche. It's not just fascinating but a valuable lesson in study about the way these minds work and the decisions they make from time to time. Success is toasted with, and failures derided. But today's euphoria dies down tomorrow when the going gets tough in later years, forcing them to abandon the same eventually. A broad look at the M&As would drive the point home. What succeeds and what goes wrong? If observed in the context, we could understand and perhaps even appreciate the decision but a critical analysis later on will unravel the crack within that gets exposed to the changing market dynamics and thus contributing to its failure.

Look closely at the timing of the M&As, the price premium paid at that time, the prevailing market dynamics and the need for the acquisition then, and how the same has played out subsequently? Every strategy is valid at that particular point of time, when viewed in the context. Several reasons also could be attributed to its failures. Cultural mismatch is one interesting issue that gets in the way of the merger between two different business entities. Viewed less seriously by many but ignoring it causes an irreconcilable difference, leading eventually to breakup. Similarly, changes in the market dynamics could also impact the marriage later. Expansion pangs affect the organizations when not thoughtfully calibrated and forecasted. Due diligence exercise must consider all these factors. Therefore, it's imperative to stay relevant, keeping pace with the changing times and customer demand.

Technology plays an important role all along and rapid changes in the same should be adhered to and dealt with in a planned and systematic manner. But with several IPs and different platforms available in the market with newer ones coming in thick and fast, the CTO and the CIO sitting together with the CEO and CMO should review them all and take a judicious call, suitable to their business and services. It's no more like, one size fits them all. Migration from the Legacy applications to the Proprietary ones is induced due to issues like Security Vulnerabilities and Compliance Challenges. The traditional linear and legacy business models are gradually conceding space to the technology/platform based model. Leveraging Technology as a Platform to do business has opened up new revenue stream for the business to adopt.

Anything that requires Process, can be and will be replaced by a machine soon. ATM is one of the examples and now Apps on our mobile phones replaced these ATMs. The high street bank branches are closing down.

Data privacy and security due diligence in M&A for technology companies are equally important.

CORPORATE COMMUNICATION: THE CORE OF MANAGEMENT

———•◎•———

Communication, though as a concept existed since the beginning of the human civilization. Various developments in global socio-political lives all through the growth of civilization and with the ubiquitous presence of ever changing technological tools, communication has assumed a new meaning and thereby much importance. In the global economy and changing world, it assumes greater significance and hence the focus.

Corporate business needs to communicate regularly to all its stakeholders – the external world and internally as well.

External: To get connected with its shareholders, customers and prospects on company's business plan, strategy, economic health, investment, goals & objectives, achievements, future business outlook and corporate social responsibility (CSR).

> *Corporate world needs to communicate regularly to all its stakeholders – the external world and internally as well.*

Internal: To keep its human resources connected with the company's larger picture, reminding them of the company's goals & objectives, enthusing them with company's achievements, advising on corporate strategy, talent management, employee engagement, business strategies, change management, business development, CSR, motivating & empowering employees through various developmental schemes, skill-set enhancement through periodic training, mentoring and business reviewing etc.

Both these factors weigh heavily on business and its positive influence on all. Corporate Communication holds an important position in the corporate structure. Effective use of this would benefit the organization in overcoming choppy times in business. The leadership management needs to understand and appreciate this and should make use of this level-playing strategic tool to its overall benefit. Ignoring the same would spell trouble in the long run and also would create uncomfortable gaps with its stakeholders. Many business leaders fail to appreciate this reducing Corporate Communication into a mere ornamental corporate mouthpiece! This fosters trust deficiency, which is detrimental to business growth.

Corporate Communication also enjoys significance in overall business perspective in the competitive world. This stitches together the related segments like Corporate Policy and Corporate Planning into the reckoning. All these are vital to the organization's overall growth and economic health. This act as a vital supporting tool while complimenting with Business Development, Sales and Customer Care, HRD and Learning & Development. This way, it plays a vital role in the corporate scheme of things. A management tool of immense value that couldn't be ignored or wished away. Prudent and planned use of communication in all its manifestation helps the company grow appreciably and in cohesion besides maintaining a strong brand image staying competitive, commanding respect in the market.

With the increase importance of communication in business, the status of Public Relations (PR) has changed fundamentally. PR has transformed itself and rechristened as Corporate Communication and has become the fulcrum of the management. It is the required connectivity that brings in the coherence among the various units of management and internal as well as external rings of activities. In other words, it brings in a sense of oneness of purpose and direction. Communication binds the company together, strengthens its resolve and energizes it to move to the future. Corporate Communication brings in a culture of management that is founded on transparency, accountability and responsiveness.

When one looks at communication holistically, it encompasses whole lot of issues to address both the external projection and internal development for business growth. The general practice by most of the business Corporate is to focus emphatically on linking up with the external world primarily for Public Relation, keeping in mind the interests of external stakeholders and shareholders. In such scenario, Corporate Communication acts as an official mouthpiece of the organization. This is definitely needed for business projection and keeping its shareholders connected while staying in touch and addressing the business dynamics. Internal communication misses out on this frenzy and gets a relatively lesser focus. Human Resource Development (HRD) department gets to be the connector with the employees. Sadly HRD, in such restricted role confines to a narrow prism and fails to play its role effectively catering largely to recruitment and training segments only. Corporate Communication could play a better and more effective role and could compliment HRD here keeping the employees connected and engaged with purpose and increasing employee's confidence in the management.

This would be appreciated more by the external world when they get to know that the human resource of the organization also feels comfortable and realises the larger corporate picture being in the same page as they are. The exercise would motivate the employees, who get into the inclusive mode in business while feeling empowered and hence, remain more productive. This is a win-win situation for both the employees and the employers. At a macro level, HRD is a subset and the welfare and resource developmental wing of Corporate Communication in the present global economy, where everyone is inter-wined and hence, inseparable. They must work in tandem, waltzing seamlessly. Captains of industries should understand this and incorporate corporate communication throughout the business cycle.

In the engagement of the employees, Corporate Communication needs to not only act as a communicator but a facilitator of their overall growth, enhancing their communication skills, knowledge development and soft-skills while interacting with the prospects and clients. This helps enhancing their intrinsic values for better market metrics. Business dynamics demand not just the domain knowledge and technical skill sets but overall improvement in the personality of the person also. This helps ascending the overall image of the organization and is perceived in a positive manner that translates into more win in business in this competitive world.

This theory is based on effective utility of individuals accruing benefit to business. If each of the members of the Corporate is a suave and erudite communicator in addition to his proficiency on relevant techno-commercial skill-sets, winning probability is higher and equally appreciated by its stakeholders. This provides the organization of the image that it strives for always, everywhere.

Many of us fail to understand and appreciate the art of communication, either internally among us within the organization or to our prospects and clients, outside. Individualism towers over and following subjective action impacts our dealings with others adversely. Be it our heavy accents, unclear uttering, whims, attitudes, inability to recognize and appreciate the audience's expectations as seen and felt through its body-language during a presentation or a business meeting – fail our communication completely. This assumes importance when the employee is not in sync with the company's overall business strategy and objectives. A simple, perceived to be a harmless ignorance or mistake could cost dearly to the organization that it could ill-afford in the competitive business scenario. Enamoured with the heady feelings of domain knowledge and technical skill-sets, we tend to ignore and give less importance to the art and science of effective communication. Objective analysis of our failures would surely point its judicious fingers at such common yet often ignored traits. Invariably and more often than not, successful leaders are good and effective communicators. It doesn't mean to mince as many words to express you to be a good communicator. Even economical verbatim with clarity in mind and logically and systematically dished out sentences in coherence with a focused aim at the calculated outcomes would ensure success. Corporate Communicator does this and should be the practice in every organization if they wish to stay above the mediocre and ahead of the competition.

The world economy has opened its doors to the global market. This demands an organization strong in foundation, leadership, clear business focus with strategies, motivated skill-sets and adaptable management. But in such multi-cultural and global competition, communication plays a vital role, connector for bridging all conceivable gaps everywhere. Organizations must realise that ineffective communication is a liability and it costs money. If communicated well internally, the outside world would be a smooth sailing. Explaining well to the outside and projecting a healthy organization would ensure business for the Corporate. Let's communicate to the world, at home and outside for win.

HUMAN RESOURCE – DEVELOPMENT?

————•◦•————

New research shows that three-quarters of gainfully employed thirty-something send out resumes and interview for new jobs at least once a year. And they leave their companies after just 28 months, on average. Some are looking for higher pay, but many who were surveyed complained that formal career development – such as mentoring and training – was lacking at their companies. Another recent survey in India conducted by CII in association with Deloitte revealed work-life, career score at the top of mind of the Gen Ys.

When companies recruit top talent, they overpromise. When giving out assignments that their new managers will find challenging and engaging, they under-deliver. But when the rubber meets the road, the mundane, tedious work process engages the soaring aspiration of the employee, demoralising him in the process.

The previously mentioned survey in India tried to understand the challenges in addressing the aspirations and concerns of a multigenerational workforce. It have an interesting but matter-of-fact observation that "Indian workplaces have become an interesting blend of three generations – the business leaders and CEOs of Baby Boomer generation (45 plus), management teams and senior professionals from Gen X (23 to 45) and young Gen Y professionals (under 23)." This generation gap has led to differences in working and communication styles as well as motivation. The study found out that the Gen Y has the "least preference for loyalty and equality, both relatively and in absolute terms."

All these development and change in perspective induces the management leadership to rethink and revisit their employee management or human resource development strategies. It needs to have a healthy blend of experience and youthful energy with innovative ideas and approaches to work. In order to avoid clashes in between, it needs to deal with each of them differently while finding out a synergy in line with the corporate objectives.

> "When Companies recruit top talent, they overpromise. When giving out assignments that their new managers will find challenging and engaging, they under-deliver."

Several fancy training modules and management theories are being practised by the new-age organizations across the globe. How many of them really benefit the people concerned and if they influence positively the working style of the management, need further probing and assessment. Kowtowing management theories by the HRD and a lack of sincerity on the part of the business leaders hamper any positive growth and the human resources continue to struggle increasing the dissatisfaction among the employees and rising attrition level. Adding misery to all these is the intolerant and the ambitious mindset of the Gen Y that doesn't espouse the age-old dictum of loyalty and adjustment. They are very clear in their mind to earn enough to enjoy a cosy lifestyle yet continuously progress and advance in career with excitement egging their emotion and moves.

Does employee engagement matter for business success?

- Sears model: 5 pt unit increase in employee attitude = 1.3 increase in customer impression = 0.5 revenue growth (*Harvard Business Review*)

- Companies where employees understand goals of their organisation have 29% greater shareholder return. *(Towers Watson)*

- Engaged employees average 2.67 days sick annually vs. 6.19 disengaged. *(Gallup)*

- Companies voted as "best to work for" yield higher returns to shareholders. *(Fortune Magazine)*

- Organisations with "engaged" employees have 6% greater return. *(McKinsey)*

- 1% of additional employee commitment is worth £200.000 in sales. *(Institute of Employment Studies)*

- 68% of customer defections are due to an indifferent employee. *(Harvard Business Review)*

Listening to the top three drivers of engagement and Focus on these will improve engagement

Blessing White Employee Engagement Research 2013 Report observes that employees in India ask for:

- *"Greater clarity about what the organisation needs me to do – and why"*

- *"Regular, specific feedback about how I'm doing"*

- *"Development opportunities and training"*

Let's put aside all preaching as espoused by several management theories and researches and look into the everyday real life that unfolds in a corporate. Most of the organizations and business houses have been making efforts at the development of the human resources through Learning & Development, Management seminars/workshops, Skill-set enhancement programs etc. But, they all struggle to contain the attrition rates. What's missing here? It is perhaps, the honest human connection and bondage, could be a sense of belongingness. The scenario also reflects the prevailing mindset of the Gen-Y that doesn't believe in loyalty and are a restless lot pursuing their ambitions within the comfort zone. When business is driven by numbers and the bottom-line demands an ever ascending graph, human resource becomes the inevitable casualty when the chips are down. Today's employees are pragmatic about the ground reality and hence, the prevalence of mistrust in between. Many a time, the custodian of employee management prefer to stay in the comfort zone and toe the management line that often borders on impersonal strategies and driven exclusively by profit, giving scant regard to human emotions.

Values and Principles in society are crumbling as are the relationships between human beings. Consumerism has spawned a breed that thrives on self-service and pursues hedonism to the hilt. Technology has brought us together but also has made us indifferent and restless. Lack of business ethics and corrupt practices have influenced many youth adversely. A cursory look into the communication and behaviour by the people in the popular social networking sites would reveal the clumsy scenario that threatens the social fabric. When the networked world spreads its reach every nook and corner of the human civilization, it strangely leaves many away from each other. This dichotomy engulfs us all today and impacts not only the social behaviour of all but the way business operates. In this mad rush, we just need to pause for introspection to fix the problem that follows us everywhere. Business needs to ride on the back of collaboration and strategy for controlled growth and the employees have to align their soaring ambition with the defined corporate objectives. Respecting each other is the crucial link in between. Even technology needs a human touch to avoid making robotic humans.

TOGETHER WE CAN!

———◉———

"Man is born free but in chains," so said Aristotle. Well, all are not 'chains'. We love to have a family and friends. Don't we? So, the individual streak inherently craves for a team spirit. The soul yearns for another and that's quite humane. Even 'Mowghli' got social with the friendly animals in the jungle.

You and I are individuals. We came alone to this world but lived with our families, in the society, within this world. Our individual identity flourished in the midst of many people. Smiles escaped the tired lips and the lifeless face glowed, when a hand held another.

We all have heard of the fictional story of how a father asked each of his seven sons (probably the poor guy was trying unsuccessfully for a daughter) to break solitary sticks and how the added up stuff was hard to attempt, acknowledging the strength of unity & togetherness. Similarly, when single fingers entwine together, they form a fist. When

> *"Individual excellence when blends with the group and they help and support each other, success cannot elude them for long. The team efforts help all, benefits all. Tasks become easier to perform and the shared endeavour evolves camaraderie and brotherhood. Collaborative efforts yield better results with less time."*

individual colors combined together, rainbow is formed. All these underlie the beauty and strength of coming together.

Heroes are the cynosure of all eyes. They are the center of all adulations. But, what will they do alone standing all by themselves, perched atop the cliff? Who will watch his heroics? Who will applaud if not seen his acts of heroism?

It's hard to dislike a hero. It's even harder to dislike an underdog. I'll share a few characters (fictional and non-fictional) with you – Luke Skywalker, Rocky Balboa, Rudy Ruettiger, Frodo Baggins, Kurt Warner and William Wallace or our home-made, Bollywood's Vijay Dinanath Chouhan or the real world mountain man - Dasrath Manjhi. Hopefully, one of these names pulls at your heart strings. The reason why is because humans are fascinated by the heroic journey. We like the overcoming of struggles and obstacles...being triumphant after vanquishing all obstacles and defeating the enemies, within and outside. We understand. We relate. We participate. We want to win as well.

Well, we need these heroes surely, to inspire several of us. We need leaders to follow. Individual excellence when blends with the group and they help and support each other, success cannot elude them for long. The team efforts help all, benefits all. Tasks become easier to perform and the shared endeavor evolves camaraderie and brotherhood. Collaborative efforts yield better results with less time.

"....focusing on Return of Engagement (ROE) rather than ROI. Instead of the 'metrics', it focused on the 'values' of social collaboration, which it concluded as profound, building better society and stronger organizations."

While working in South Africa, I was deputed to Khartoum city in Sudan to boost the sagging morale of my software engineers working in a local government project. I was there for continuous six months and worked with the team to not only help them complete the project before time but also begging more business with my team's support and help. We triumphed together and the team spirit got us closer to each other with a stronger bonding. This is one of the several such gratifying moments in my professional life. I revel in my team spirit as I am a complete team man.

More often than not, the 'I' is more pronounced than the 'WE', leading to all social strife and tension in relationships. The 'Selfie' is symptomatic of the malady that the present generation is afflicted with and hence, breakdowns in all relations with a burgeoning one-upmanship in the career and social strata. Resurgence of the overpowering ego and self-serviced individualism kills the spirit of unity and team work.

Many businesses and even start-ups have bitten the dust along the way only due to this individual conflict and ego clashes. Absence of mutual respect is a lethal anomaly that demolishes unity and togetherness. Trust and mutual respect are vital in all relationships and a strong unwavering commitment to staying together could only brave all challenges and possible negative emotions. When in a group, if we ignore the shortcomings of our fellow colleagues/partners and instead utilize and concentrate on their strengths, complementing each other finding synergies, we will succeed. We must agree to disagree as well. If one believes in relationships, maintaining the same and working hard to keep it alive, rest on the people involved. Unity demands trust and respect besides investing in patience and working towards its success. Ego, arrogance, domineering, disrespectful and being argumentative are the vices that would surely pull down the labored edifice. It's imperative that people venturing into businesses must keep these in mind and enter into an unquestionable agreement in between and treat it as a sacred document...a Bible...a Gita.

Of course, individual leaders have always led the crowd but revolutions are won when the people come together and the collective force pulls down the mighty autocrats and enemies of civilization from their lavish thrones. Organizations and associations are made of individuals with collective vision and willing to work together towards the envisioned objectives and goal. Drops of water make an ocean.

Life is celebrated better in a group rather than alone. Sports teams and the armed forces revel in collective effort and team work. It gives a different joy when one person gets support from the other to complete the task at hand with a smile on the face. The shared vision gets accomplished in a collaborative effort.

KPMG in one of its research documents on Enterprise Social Networking (ESN) has very interestingly suggested focusing on Return of Engagement (ROE) rather than ROI. Instead of the 'metrics', it focused on the 'values' of social collaboration, which it concluded as profound, building better society and stronger organizations. Facebook evolved greatly around this theme of togetherness in a global social milieu of engagement.

Coming Together is the Beginning, Keeping Together is the Process; Working Together is Success. Because, **Together WE Can!**

MANAGING CHANGE

———◦○◦———

Leaders need to be on the lookout for what today's rapidly changing business landscape means to them and their organizations. It is vital to assess change readiness first. Changes are required at periodic intervals for strategic values and plans. It is inevitable either for the growth trajectory or to enhance competitive quotient.

Post a merger and/or acquisition, there seem to have been heartburns among a section of employees disturbing the equation within and destabilizing the prevalent set up within the organization. It is pure human nature to resist change. A prejudiced mind, negative perceptions and apprehensions create innumerable challenges for the management to deal with as a consequence. Absence of clear communication compounds the misery. First of all, the leadership management should assess the compatibility issues before effecting the changes to align them with the defined corporate objectives while clarifying all on the strategy. They should take the Corporate Communication and Human Resource departments into confidence to gear up for the

> *"The wind of change that is sweeping across India today and in several parts of the world earlier was symptomatic of a repressed citizenry with regressed rules of law. It just needs a common rallying point or cause to cling onto moving along the way to its assorted collective aspirations."*

perceived scenario and should come out with thoughtful strategy and clear and targeted communication. Together with the Learning & Development department, they all should devise plans to reach out to all employees with clear and unambiguous information.

In order to manage such changes, Change Agents are required to campaign and the management should form a team comprising selective key team members from across the board. They will keep the flock together and this will ensure support from team members while engaging the cynical. However, necessary plans need to be mooted not to disturb the continuing process and business and to retain the best talents, even if some don't fit into the scheme of things in the changed scenario. This will send a very positive and appreciative message across the organization.

It is always easy said than done to deal with the complex human nature, whose mind is wired against changes. Unless convinced on the purpose of the same and if that doesn't benefit them, they would continue to create challenges and could even vitiate the atmosphere by indulging in rumours.

Take the example of implementing Enterprise Resource Planning (ERP) in organizations that has been happening for so long and so frequently. This defines the system and outlines a clear process but if not seamlessly aligned to the followed business model and the domain it engages in, it would utterly fail in its attempt and compound the misery going along with the inherent human nature (of resisting change). There have been several instances of such failures of ERP implementation in many organizations across the world. When ERP entered into the market initially, the promoters of the same just tried to impose them as off-the-shelf product to thrust on them and shove it down their grumbling throat. The consequences were too risky and far reaching to handle, resulting in total collapse of the same and wastage of precious dollars. Experience and business prudence have changed the approach now making it more professional and with detailed integration process even prior to its implementation. In order to manage the changes and in anticipation of resistance within and disturbance of business flow, there has been a very thoughtful marriage between the implementer and the end-user client. More often than not, the ERP producing company encourages involvement of highly professional consulting companies to act as a go-between and implementer of the software effectively and systematically managing all possible challenges. This has ensured success and easy integration with the prevailing business processes. The practice reflects on the fundamentals of Change Management principle.

Let's review such a scenario in the society or in a country. Unless the same principles of changed management are followed with thoughtful planning keeping alive a clear communication channel, it would be well neigh impossible to come out unscathed. The dreaded fall-out could be devastating and irreparable. The wind of change that is sweeping across India today and in several parts of the world earlier was symptomatic of a repressed citizenry with regressed rules of law. It just needs a common rallying point or cause to cling onto moving along the way to its assorted collective aspirations. It might succeed and could bring about the desired change toppling the hostile incumbent but the challenges start right after. Burdened with high expectation and expecting to be different, the ensuing exercise gets tougher when the ground reality offers a not so conducive atmosphere. Many a times, the leaders struggle to keep the flock together and at times buckle under the pressure and collapse eventually. Hence, it is prudent to be proactively prepared with possible challenges in anticipation with a clear and structured strategy and plan of action. It is equally important to keep a team of key members ready to campaign for effectively warding off cynicism but with pragmatic approach. It all requires effective leadership qualities and professional management.

SQUEEZED BETWEEN TOP-LINE & BOTTOM-LINE GROWTH!

———•◦◉◦•———

It's the first day in office and as a part of the Induction program; I was going through the rituals meeting and listening to various senior executives of the organization. The last day was with the CMD of the company, who always gives this privilege to talk to the senior management professionals. We all new entrants huddled around the large oval shaped table and couched into the swivel chairs. Waiting with excitement we got engaged in some friendly banter, relaxing a bit after going through the routines that many of us have experienced and even conducted over few decades.

> *"Our lives are always on the move and we most of the times live out of the suitcase, constantly chasing about the target that hangs over our heads permanently. The question is not about the working environment but the expected dedication and round-the-clock job schedules."*

There walked in the CMD's PA smiling at everyone and looking around before the 'Boss' comes in. Few minutes later the EA to CMD trooped in with his assistance to oversee the arrangements. He looked at us with a customary grin hanging loose on his chubby face. He nods at the PA and whispers into his ear signaling his satisfaction at the arrangements. PA walks out before keeping the personal accompanying tools and gadgets of the CMD on the appointed space on the table. The EA waved at us with that look of superiority. Couple of the guys walked up to him shaking hands in a buddy-buddy manner. After all Boss's team carry same aura and respect from many. The large door opened up and the CMD with PA in toe marched in. Everyone got up. Suddenly the room came to life. The shiny face of the CMD released a smile that found instant echo from the people around. The studied silence got ruptured with a chorus – "good morning Sir". He reciprocated and occupied his chair, the largest among the furniture placed in the middle. The guy next to me was the first to speak up to the Boss, asking how he was and spoke in praise in their common tongue. Perhaps, he's signaling to others how close he could be to the Boss. The CMD got up. Gulped down water in a jiffy and started the customary exchange of pleasantries. He started his presentation on the wall mounted 50" LCD explaining company's goals and objectives peppered as usual with some pep talk and priding in his journey along. He paused and glanced over his shoulder to ever-nodding senior executives around. He smiled but spoke in a tone firm in resolution and authority asking if everyone has got its Blackberry handsets. A chorus erupted in unison in the affirmative, many even flaunting the gleaming tiny device in hand. The CMD went on to explain the reason the company has spent money for this. He said that it's given so that each of us is available for job 24x7. The smiling faces changed its countenance, looking in askance at each other. He added that we should be able to balance our work-life schedules but he doesn't care if the work demands your attention even at odd hours of the day or night. People should be prepared to travel anywhere with even an hour's notice. This, he said requires everyone to have his bags ready with all minimum necessary belongings and should be kept in toe in the office itself. The ones not belonging to the Business Development functions frowned. The whip descended on pulling them out of their cocoon. He then went on to exhort all to give their best for the development of the organization and with a very subtle yet stern voice advised all to contribute sincerely to the bottom-line while constantly keeping the top-line in the ascending order.

Well, this is just an innocuous sermon that we all have experienced in the corporate life. It's perhaps nothing new and not much to deliberate about for the seasoned Sales & Business Development professionals. Our lives are always on the move and we most of the times live out of the suitcase, constantly chasing about the target that hangs over our heads permanently. The question is not about the working environment but the expected dedication and round-the-clock job schedules. Now, how does such a person manage his personal or family life, leave aside his hobbies or mundane passions? Remember, at the end-of-the-day no one is indispensable. Expectant job seekers are constantly available. Hire & fire or replacing you with another is the rule of the game. If not you, it's someone else. To be fair to him, the entrepreneur has to not only increase business and profit but these days, has to keep the investors constantly happy about. He's already sucked into this never-ending race for better results and increased share value in the market. Contentment is not a sacred parenthesis for him. He's perched on the ever-running tread mill that expects the walker to move ahead always. Unfortunately, this machine doesn't offer a slow-down button and switching off is like taking to the path of penance in the Himalayas. This is his predicament!

The question that goes begging is why do most business men crowd out their lounges with so many hands when the going gets smooth and displace the same ones at the show of panic in the business? A prudent foresight would save the blushes later on. Look at how the government PSUs in India is saddled with, making them ineffective and salary consuming behemoths. A leaner and horses for the courses population would make planning easier and effective not straining on the exchequer. The private companies commit the same mistakes. The resultant casualties always are the poor employees. Barring a few (particularly in the Indian context) businessmen most tend to use and throw their human resources. Unfortunately, in many of the cases the custodian of people, the HRD works hand-in-glove in such scenarios like the spineless bureaucrats kow-towing the mindless decisions of the unimaginative politicians.

The rhetoric about human resource development gets a lip-service in many organizations and majority times gets confined to the plus environs of the five-star hotels hosting corporate seminars and workshops. Reams of pages and countless slides are devoted to sing paean on the efficacy of and importance of human resource. The rhetoric gets missed out and buries itself in the heap of number game every quarter. It all boils down to "billable components". The jigsaw puzzle that enumerates between the topline and bottom-line growth leaves no space for the human factor. Everything gets reduced to numbers. One's fate resides on his generated numbers. You are 'valued' with this number and your worth defines the same.

From business point of view this looks and sounds absolutely sacrosanct and perhaps logical in view of the money spent. There is no room for a non-performer as no company could afford to carry along passengers only. Everyone has its roles and responsibilities well defined (well at least as far as the expectations are concerned) and deliverables made equally clear. Everyone has to and should contribute if not in equal measure at least in equal enthusiasm and sincerity towards the growth of the organization. This is agreed fully without question asked. But looking from the social responsibility context, business also has a social perspective. If I have selected you and you are performing if not exceeding in expectations, I have a responsibility towards you and I just can't treat you as a commodity (to use & throw). From the author's experience, it's seen that majority of employees are sincere enough in their jobs. Given proper guidance and encouragement, they would surely live

> *"Business can't just be seen through an onerous prism of money creation. The value perspective needs to factor in the human context as well and the dignity that the job entails for them."*

to the expectations. What's a leader if he can't groom his team and just goes with star performers. There will always be the second and third rung. Managers (Leaders) with the help of HRD should identify these and help device a program for their skill enhancement (Learning & Development is doing this). Talk to them in private and take them into confidence by entrusting larger jobs and including them in your important assignments, map out their contributions in small measures (leaving the larger & critical ones to your trusted performers). Make them a part of the winning team and see how they change themselves in such scenarios. Taste of success and the recognition thereon would spur their flagging morale and would egg them to improve (& to be with the winning team always). Nothing succeeds like success. This will surely change the once laggard guys to performers, at times exceeding the targets. You don't need formulas with human-being always. Appeal to their emotions and boost their confidence by leading from the front. Be with them always (even in their personal crisis) and they will be with you forever. It's not just money but humane values and respect that pay off.

There is another peculiar phenomenon perhaps seen in Indian family run business context (prevalent more in the Infrastructure domain) where, the mind-set dithers professional values. Business can't just be seen through an onerous prism of money creation. The value perspective needs to factor in the human context as well and the dignity that the job entails for them. Economic recessions and when the chips are down in one-off instances are understandable but beyond schedule salary disbursement (most of the times) for the employees and not clearing pending dues (full & final settlement) of the ones, who've resigned from the services for months together (at times years on with cajoling & at times through legal claims) amount to criminal offence and disrespecting human values and professional ethics. These are the two very disturbing developments that are plaguing some of the industry houses in this part of the world. A stronger HRD would help subverting such irregularities. For many of the readers, this would be news but for some it is the unfortunate truth as they or their friends and cousins might have experienced. No wonder such news is swept under the carpet and not many express them in public. There still are such writings in private blogs and when one tries to Google about it in the internet. Readers often ignore them as a case of sour grapes!

The saving grace is not all could be painted in the same brush. Not all organizations suffer from such devious practices. I am just talking about the few black-sheep who are giving the industry a bad name and some sleepless nights to its unfortunate employees. There would surely be improvement in such scenarios if the leadership management genuinely respects human resource as THE key factor in the success of business.

We salute the organizations and its leadership management, who deservingly get voted as the Best Organizations to work for or as the Best Employers. Not only business but the country as a whole would prosper with a happy and satisfied worker/employee. Genuine development of the employees and respect for their personal lives would surely restrict and arrest attrition rates in the industry, of course, besides an exciting growth prospect and challenging environment. That completes the ideal organization but when imperfections are the rule and such thoughts are considered utopian, the battle goes on and issues debated. The fence on the other side always looks greener. Hop on for an experience. Sing along if happy but join me if not.

WORKPLACE STRESS: THE NEW-ECONOMY KILLER

Aseem and Ankita are just a couple of years married young couple, working since almost a decade in two top MNCs in the silicon Valley of India, Bangalore where couple of thousands young job aspirants land up for jobs every day from across India. No wonder, the city is bursting at its seam in all spheres. Both of them are typical upwardly mobile yuppies, following in the footsteps of their ilk, which believes in 'working hard and partying harder.' While completely engrossed in their professional activities, they are equally active in all other things of their choices. Life has been a breeze and the young couple have had great times together. Slogging for a minimum of 8-10 hours every day inside the cosy offices in shifts and returning home to continue the same with laptops and headphones through late in the nights, matching with the international time zones. The much favoured 'work from home' became a fad, a simple extension of the same work schedule. Running endlessly behind the set deadlines, they become workaholics. They turn into human machines, robots- sacrificing sleep and a normal life. Life changes for the couple and this starts affecting their lifestyle, moods and health. Sleep deprivation turns to sleep apnoea, leading to several health disorders and mood swings. Irritability rules their conversations and arguments affecting their relationships. Their happy-go-lucky lives turn sour. Supplements of all kinds of medicines to escape the stress related symptoms get into their daily intakes. Regular use of pleasure intoxicants with erratic lifestyle and too much mental as well physical stress gets a telling effect on their psyche and health. Aseem and Ankita are a different couple today... far from their lovey-dovey lives. Today, they are visiting for counselling with the psychiatrists. Respective families and friends are concerned. But, the couple doesn't relent. They continue to be sucked into the rigmarole of corporate grime, in dogged pursuance of career growth with a lifestyle that is driven by crass consumerism. Well, this is how our society today is. And they are not the only couple showing the disturbing symptoms of job stress and early burnouts, but are just part of several thousands, exhibiting the same stress levels and anxiety. India's working demography has changed considerably today and we have a growing pool of completely stressed out and burnt out youngsters. Does this bode well for our society? No, it doesn't. But why does this happen and how do we address this? Who is responsible and what's to be done to arrest the sliding? So many questions dog our agitated minds. Let's look for the possible answers while scanning the scenario and dissecting the issues concerned.

> *"Pressure at the workplace is unavoidable due to the demands of the contemporary work environment. Deadlines have to be met without excuse. There is a strong accountability in place in the corporate sector. Pressure is inevitable to maintain discipline. There is high competition all around, in the market and inside the workplace. There is absolutely no room for complacency and error."*

Corporate Life

My Boss used to tell me often, "Don't sit on the Pressure...Pass it on." To supplement his advice, he used to explain how he is under pressure from the Management and so has to put me under the same and I should follow suit. This cycle actually rolls on daily in the private sector job corridors. Ask anyone, he will only nod in agreement.

Employees get sandwiched between the top-line and bottom-line growth charts. Yes, today's business is all about the Numbers. One cannot escape it so long as she/he is "Billable".

Pressure at the workplace is unavoidable due to the demands of the contemporary work environment. Deadlines have to be met without excuse. There is a strong accountability in place in the corporate sector. Pressure is inevitable to maintain discipline. There is high competition all around, in the market and inside the workplace. There is absolutely no room for complacency and error. The joke that used to make rounds in the corporate gossip corridors- "To Err is Human but the Company doesn't have a Policy of Forgiving." Pressure perceived as acceptable by an individual, may even keep workers alert, motivated, able to work and learn, depending on the available resources and personal characteristics. However, when the individual coping mechanism fails to handle the events, pressure builds up. And when pressure becomes excessive or otherwise unmanageable it leads to stress. Stress can damage an employees' health and the business performance.

What is Work-Related Stress?

"One reason for burnouts, anxiety, and depression is that people, who are obsessively passionate, tie their self-worth to outcomes that are often outside their control and limit. Passion can both be a gift and a curse, depending on the use and the goals attached."

- Work-related stress is the response people may have when presented with work demands and pressures that are not matched to their knowledge and abilities and which challenge their ability to cope.

- Stress occurs in a wide range of work circumstances but is often made worse when employees feel they have little support from supervisors and colleagues, as well as little control over work processes.

- There is often confusion between pressure or challenge and stress and sometimes it is used to excuse bad management practice.

Work-related stress can be caused by poor work organisation (the way we design jobs and work systems, and the way we manage them), by poor work design (for example, lack of control over work processes), poor management, unsatisfactory working conditions, and lack of support from colleagues and supervisors.

Research findings show that the most stressful type of work is that which values excessive demands and pressures that are not matched to workers' knowledge and abilities, where there is little opportunity to exercise any choice or control, and where there is little support from others.

Employees are less likely to experience work-related stress when - demands and pressures of work are matched to their knowledge and abilities - control can be exercised over their work and the way they do it - support is received from supervisors and colleagues - participation in decisions that concern their jobs is provided.

What are Stress-Related Hazards at Work?

Stress related hazards at work can be divided into work content and work context.

Work contents includes - job content (monotony, under-stimulation, meaningless of tasks, lack of variety, etc) - work load and work pace (too much or too little to do, work under time pressure, etc.) - working hours (strict or inflexible, long and unsocial, unpredictable, badly designed shift systems) - Participation and control (lack of participation in decision-making, lack of control over work processes, pace, hours, methods, and the work environment)

Work context includes - career development, status and pay (job insecurity, lack of promotion opportunities, under- or over-promotion, work of ‹low social value›, piece rate payment schemes, unclear or unfair performance evaluation systems, being over- or under-skilled for a job)

- role in the organization (unclear role, conflicting roles) - interpersonal relationships (inadequate, inconsiderate or unsupportive supervision, poor relationships with colleagues, bullying/harassment and violence, isolated or solitary work, etc) -organizational culture (poor communication, poor leadership, lack of behavioural rule, lack of clarity about organizational objectives, structures and strategies) - work-life balance (conflicting demands of work and home, lack of support for domestic problems at work, lack of support for work problems at home, lack of organizational rules and policies to support work-life balance)

What's Making One so Stressed?

At first glance, it might seem pretty obvious why the workplace is making you so stressed out - it's work! However, there are very specific triggers for the kind of stress you're experiencing at the office. In a StressPulse survey by EAP provider ComPsych, workers listed the following reasons as their main causes for stress.

- People related issues (28%)
- Work Load (46%)
- Work Life balance (20%)
- Lack of Job Security (6%)
- Feeling constantly connected to office
- Not getting enough hours/Working too late

One reason for burnouts, anxiety, and depression is that people, who are obsessively passionate, tie their self-worth to outcomes that are often outside their control and limit. Passion can both be a gift and a curse, depending on the use and the goals attached.

While doing the research on this subject, this author had interacted with several youngsters who have just started their professional career in various companies, narrating their situations that have stressed them out, many of whom are quitting jobs and changing companies frequently. Two issues became apparent here,

A. Lack of proper guidance and preparedness from their passed out colleges (not making them industry ready). They have bookish knowledge only but no minimum work knowledge/understanding, including about the basic corporate rules and regulations, besides the working styles, work culture and work assignments. These greenhorns are not fully equipped with the prevailing technologies, skillsets and thus find the going tough considerably.

B. Not many companies conduct the initial Induction Programme sincerely. And the seniors simply throw these rookies into the grind, assigning tight schedules and deadlines with not much guidance and handholding. Several small and medium level companies are very unprofessionally managed with HR being the weakest link in them. In such unfortunate scenario, work suffers, productivity declines and attrition increases. No wonder, many Indian companies fail to remain competitive in business and don't sustain longer in the market.

This is not a healthy sign for the country and begs for urgent attention. Corporate HR and L&D professionals must pay attention to this rapidly growing malaise and devise necessary mechanisms, sensitising the seniors and the management, while empathising especially with these new recruits. Yes, this prevails in several overseas MNCs as well.

Though not gender specific but women get more affected with job stress due to social traditions in which, they have more share of domestic responsibilities like child bearing and rearing. Longer maternity breaks also impact their career. It's much more difficult for the women when saddled with job anxiety.

> "In the pursuit of material progress and consumerism, gradual decay in family value systems has been noticed since over last two decades. This has been puncturing the social fabric with all-round spill over effects. Parenting has to be faulted with for this disturbing change."

Career Ambition

Today's youth is completely career focused and ambition driven. Good for them actually but as long as this doesn't capture their complete attention, side-lining other aspects in life. Personal and social relationships flounder when the undivided attention focuses overly on ambition for career only. The late marriage, nucleus family and single child or no child phenomenon stem from this trend. This has surely changed the social fabric where individualism reigns supreme over family and community feelings. The resultant human behaviour tends to tilt heavily towards an indifferent and self-focussed tribe that becomes narcissist and self-centred. To defend and justify this, we tend to speak about the changing times and fast paced life. This, according to the social scientists, manifests aversion to taking personal responsibilities beyond one's own family (husband, wife & kid) and is a form of modern day social escapism.

Being workaholic certainly is not a prized trophy to be flaunted but a menace that could annihilate human spirit and joy hence, needs careful attention and as much avoidance.

Millennial Psyche & Social Milieu

Impetuosity rules the restless minds of the millennial. Adjusting to different environment, away from their comfort zones is not their strength. Spoon fed or overly protected by the doted parents during their childhood from complex situations, they are a vulnerable lot when facing challenges in life later on. They tend to break down invariably under stress. It is better to make them aware of and make them experience such situations in a regulated manner at least, during the formative years. This will help them coping up with the challenges in career and personal life, later on. Protectionism makes people weak, because in the absence of it, they wouldn't know how to handle the situation. The demographic divide is quite visible in this context, wherein an economically weaker boy behaves differently and with much control in comparison with his richer peers, when it comes to deal with life's challenges.

Family Values

Families are the major source of love and support. It nurtures the young members with certain values and discipline that continues with them all through. Thus, it is important to have such value systems to inculcate. All these shape up the persons and mould the personalities. A stronger foundation would help in withstanding challenges ahead. Absence of the same would break them down under duress. Emotional support from the family helps tremendously in trying times. The support members in the family must lend empathy and should try to soothe the frayed nerves. Love and affections work wonders. This emotional juice must flow uninterrupted. Family support system would offer strength and peace to the beleaguered soul. In the pursuit of material progress and consumerism, gradual decay in family value systems has been noticed since over last two decades. This has been puncturing the social fabric with all-round spill over effects. Parenting has to be faulted with for this disturbing change.

"According to the study conducted by the World Health Organization (WHO), around 200 million people in India may suffer from depression i.e. one in five people. No wonder, we are one of the most depressed countries in the world, as per another WHO study."

Health Issues & Clinical Analysis

As health is not merely the absence of disease or infirmity but a positive state of complete physical, mental and social well-being (WHO, 1986), a healthy working environment is one in which there is not only an absence of harmful conditions but an abundance of health-promoting ones

Corporate stress is the new killer. Burnout stress is the worst kind of stress with symptoms of complete physical, emotional and mental exhaustion which comes as a result of the pursuit of, more often than not, unattainable goals that pushes to the limit and beyond.

Signs that you are dealing with some serious stress:

- You constantly feel anxious or depressed
- You're easily irritated, whether at work or at home
- You suffer from fatigue, but you have a hard time sleeping
- You find it difficult to concentrate or stay focused
- You feel apathetic about things that once interested you
- You're getting sick much more often
- You've experienced a sudden dip in your sex drive
- You've been turning to alcohol, drugs, or both to deal with the stress

Sociological Analysis

Happiness quotient is linked to a healthy nation, deciding its productivity and progression. On the other hand, a stressed out human resource loses the demographic dividends. With growing attrition rates in the private companies, increasing divorce cases, neurological issues, alcoholism among the younger population as a result of stress and early burnouts, have negatively impacted the families, society and the nation. All these have influenced the gross human productivity that has a socio-economic fall out. Today, the Sociologists are alarmed at the rapid growth of an unhappy population and family break downs. This is also one of the reasons of the ascending crime graphs today. Frequent mood swings elicit extreme behaviour, leading to violent acts at times. Career ambitions for many and hedonistic pleasure for some, drive the lives to the extreme. Relationships become the biggest casualty to all these, puncturing the social fabric invariably. The youthful impetuosity doesn't give a struggling relationship any chance. Emotions get hammered in the process resulting in break-downs in relationships at all level. This alters the social fabric irreparably, which is not a healthy situation to be in. Materialism and consumerism have surely provoked people to nurse such desires.

According to the study conducted by the World Health Organization (WHO), around 200 million people in India may suffer from depression i.e. one in five people. No wonder, we are one of the most depressed countries in the world, as per another WHO study. There could be many reasons for why "Mental Health" is not taken seriously by the Indians with usual indifference, lack of empathy and even social stigmas attached more often, which could try to sweep the issues under the carpet or not being taken seriously.

Emotional Quotient

Perspective is limited to her/his position while that of the employer is wider and bigger. The former is only answerable to her/his employers (immediate superior/reporting authority), while the leadership management have to think of all related stakeholders and shareholders. Larger listed companies tend to climb up the one way ladder that doesn't allow or appreciate sliding downs. All these have spiral effects and thus, the endless pressures. Educational institutions would do well to impart training to its students on EQ and Life Skills to save burn outs later. The other issue is that of the gaps between the expectations (of the employees) and the demands (from jobs), which when mismatches, create emotional strife and frustrations. Patience is never the strength of the youth and loyalty becomes a casualty often. The restless youthful souls seek escape routes exploring changes but every time when the novelty wears off, they struggle with the same situation.

PRESCRIPTIONS TO ESCAPE, ADJUST, CHANGE... OR ABANDON?

Recognition and respect at work: a fundamental human need

Being respected and appreciated by significant others is one of the most fundamental human desire. Consequently, people go to great pain to gain acceptance and approval. Recent research in the domain of occupational health psychology shows that many stressful experiences are linked to being offended – for instance, by being offended or ridiculed, by social exclusion, by social conflict, by illegitimate tasks. Such experiences of being treated in an unfair manner constitute an "Offence to Self", and this may have quite far reaching consequences in terms of health and well-being. Conversely, being appreciated is one of the most important factors that increase motivation and satisfaction as well as health and well-being.

The Ethos

Ethos or certain life principles drive the person in her/his life's journey. Lack of it will take the steam out from the sail. A sense of Pride and Ownership has to be imbibed to move along the path with purpose and vigour. This is vital to a person's self-esteem. Absence of the same would create the vacuum and thus, irritability and negativity.

Human beings are not machines. They are made of flesh and blood, thus possess emotions and their body reacts that could lead to much wear and tear. Human touch, compassion, empathy and team spirit impact the human psyche positively and help them cope up with the pressure.

Of course, professionalism demands discipline and adapting to the situations. Fierce business competition has impacted the bottom-line margins and this impels less room for any lapses and tight schedules. It is challenging nevertheless but the new economy has to survive despite the prevalent hostile conditions. This is the dichotomy today though not fully justified and cannot be defended at the cost of neglecting the valuable human resources.

Considering these factors, a holistic approach is needed to address this disturbing trend that threatens India's much flaunted demographic dividends. This young nation could be ailing fast and unless handled with care, could slide into mass depression and mental disorder, turning this into an alarming new economy killer. Stress afflicted minds need to train their brains to face and overcome challenges in life and reboot their fledgling career, maintaining emotional balance at the work place and at home.

HR ANALYTICS & BUSINESS PROCESS

———•◉•———

Evolution is a process that defines the progress of civilization pushing the boundary beyond. Human beings along their journey transform and evolve. Organizations are also trying to keep pace with the changing environment and competition is keeping them on their toes.

"The challenge of HR Analytic is to identify what data should be captured and how to use the data to model and predict capabilities so that the organization gets an optimal return on investment (ROI) on its human capital."

Business process and strategies have been trying to utilize all the resources available to the maximum extent. Market dynamics is driving both the business and the practitioners and its consumers along with the enablers.

Striving for excellence and to stay ahead in the race, organizations are on a competitive mission to unravel the human potential that could transform their businesses. Humongous data are being elicited in the whole processes involving the human resource as business enablers and drivers. Human Resource (HR) today is trying to analyse the data being unfolded to understand human behaviour while measuring their potential towards better productivity and performance. Strategy is now being aligned with through the Data Analytic (DA) to reach business goals quickly and effectively.

The challenge of HR Analytic is to identify what data should be captured and how to use the data to model and predict capabilities so that the organization gets an optimal return on investment (ROI) on its human capital. Various technological tools are being used and deployed towards this topping with Business Intelligence (BI) or Data Federation Technology. Data mining and Business Analytic techniques are linked to HR data. Various tools and methods are being examined and evaluated for use.

After all it is the influenced human behaviour and imbibed skill-sets with gradual learning and acquired education that set the stage open and complicated for the managers to handle. In order to make the human resource effective, would technology help or tapping on the humane aspect would? Researchers and HR professionals have been busy tapping this for better and effective utilization of human resources and various skill set improvement training plans have been mooted. It's an equal challenge for the L&D community to devise relevant training. India surely has woken up to this new found means towards better business and effective use of the human resource. When attrition levels are so high and business dynamics are so uncertain, investment in such a laborious exercise shouldn't drain the patience levels among the entrepreneurs. Efficacy of HR Analytic as a very important tool in business development for the organization has been understood and appreciated. Sincerity in the exercise would benefit them all but the action has just begun and the verdict is yet to be out in the open. An exciting journey begins and we await the same getting unfold soon. Keep the big data crunching, the churning of it would get the organizations the eureka moment conjoining artificial intelligence and business analytic. The combined tools would make them stronger and ahead of the competition.

According to Deloitte's recent Global Human Capital Trends 2014 report, 86% of companies report no analytics capabilities in the HR function and 67% rate themselves as weak at using HR data to predict workforce performance and improvement. About 85 % of respondents of Economist Intelligence Unit survey of 418 global executives commissioned by KPMG International said their HR team did not excel at providing insightful and predictive analytics that could have a positive impact on the success of the organization. This not only points at the inherent limitations but perhaps exposes the glaring absence of deploying relevant methods. Google, for example, is ahead of the curve when it comes to people data. The company developed a comprehensive database that captured information about current employees' attitude, behaviour, personality and job performance. This data subsequently enabled Google to develop an algorithm for predicting which applicants were most likely to succeed.

Experts and advocates of HR Data Analytics opine for a collaborative efforts between the key internal stakeholders of the organizations towards business development and growth. There ought to be synergy among HR and Corporate Communication along with its subset L&D with a dotted line to Business Development. The latter being the bottom-line of all business venture and the growing emphasis on making the employees "billable" (as is often called in the IT industry), understanding of business and its complete process would help HR and L&D leaders devising their functional strategies. Gone are the days when departments within the organization worked in a water-tight compartment and many a times working in isolation. All efforts and activities now boil down to the development of business and top-line growth of the organization with a healthy bottom-line (profit margins).

This collaborative effort could foster camaraderie as well as utilize the talents as per their strengths and not harping on their weaknesses. Attrition could be nipped in the bud, if attention is pared among these elements. But it's equally challenging for these functional groups coming together and working in tandem. The underlying current of domain and functional 'egos' pose hurdles in the way. The often brandied question of who's more important in the business process: production & engineering or sales & marketing or HR & L&D or finance & accounting, would play spoilsport in this process. Murmurs inside the corridors of corporate alleys have gained momentum wide in the open. Today, there have been discussions and debates on who should be the CEO of the organization belonging to which functionality? Members of each of these groups stake their argued claims.

Hence, merely collecting and collating enough data wouldn't serve the purpose. Knowing which data to work on and understanding of complete business would help in linking up the efforts to the growth trajectory that the organizations aim at every quarter.

In essence, what is needed is a connected and coherent, objective-driven approach that articulates and puts in operation the collaboration. This would help closing the gap between strategy and daily operations thus, making the efforts effective and successful.

In view of the changing market dynamics and growing competitions, it's now imperative to have good understanding of the business processes and insight into each of the functions within, would help the CEO to wade through the choppy corporate waters.

Hope lingers in the inquisitive minds and explanations are being brandied about by the votaries of various theories. But the occurrences and various developments around the world in the corporate world offer a strong glimpse of collaborative effort and strategic moves.

E-COMMERCE: RE-TAILING TO E-TAILING

---•◎•---

Social media is one of the main reasons behind India's 250 million people being online. Availability and use of mobile phones particularly the new-age Android types, help staying connected with the world 24x7. Today India is among the top six Internet Economies in the world. The market is too big for the retailers and business houses to ignore.

> "The advent of e-commerce is a great fillip to the overall consumerism story in India. The success of Flipkart, Jabong and Snapdeal clearly shows that there is no absence of demand. E-commerce is clearly fuelling customer acquisition in India."

Having the online shop window seems to work for the brands. It's not just phones and garments — the broader retail business is opting for a similar online-only strategy.

Entering the Indian market through e-tailers gives brands a wider reach along with faster delivery which will help the brand reach out to the target audience across cities in India.

Brands are gravitating to online first because it helps them avoid expenses associated with brick-and-mortar, such as steep rents and high distribution costs, particularly with e-commerce making rapid gains in terms of customer acquisition.

Starting a brick-and-mortar outlet in India has many challenges such as the high rental estate costs, low sale density and difficult scalability. Online gives you quick reach even in those pockets where you are unable to open physical stores.

Seven-year-old flipkart.com, the country's largest e-commerce site, clocked $1 billion (Rs 6,100 crore) in sales in the current fiscal year, a year ahead of target. That's about twice the expected sales of Shoppers Stop (BSE 2.31%), the country's largest listed department store operator that started business 23 years ago. That's why organised retail, from supermarket chains to apparel store operators, has major e-commerce ambitions. Online sales are expected to grow about eight times to $8 billion in the next six years, primarily fuelled by hundreds of millions of internet accessing mobile phone subscribers.

The advent of e-commerce is a great fillip to the overall consumerism story in India. The success of Flipkart, Jabong and Snapdeal clearly shows that there is no absence of demand. E-commerce is clearly fuelling customer acquisition in India. eBay and Amazon have their eyes clearly trained on the vast Indian market.

That's why retailers and brands are encouraged to start selling online even if they don't have a physical store presence in India. The growth of online retailing is of great concern to traditional modern retailers as well as mall operators. Earlier, consumers would generally conduct initial product research online before buying goods from physical stores. The trend seems to have reversed now. The trend is known as 'showrooming' — consumers seek to experience products in brick-and-mortar stores before looking online for the cheapest price. That's prompting many retailers and mall owners to consider making the migration themselves.

Consumer goods (mostly electronics), fashion garments and snacks (Pizzas & Burgers) have joined the bandwagon already and the young Indian shoppers have embraced this new trend.

However, some experts are sceptical about an online-first strategy as globally companies tend to build brands through brick-and-mortar stores before taking them online. Companies serious about a long-term business are wondering about their business strategy in view of this surge in online purchase. There surely is a paradigm shift in the consumer choice and preference. As it happens, the traditional market feels threatened, though puts up a brave front now. Old order changes, yielding to the new...riding on the twin emotions of scepticism and hope!

A new trend comes with its untested hiccups. E-tailers have little solution for demand spikes. The "Big Billion Sale" debacle of Flipkart when stocks disappeared within seconds, cancellation of orders and website crashing leaving the consumers high & dry offered ample concern among these players and doubts in the minds of the consumers. It's agreed that e-tailers cannot accept orders without thinking about logistics issues. Seasonal shopping experiences higher demand. The e-commerce world must analyse and gear up to the uncertain and erratic ways of consumer behaviour at the beginning of a new trend. Things would be better off once the dust settles down.

The buzz is on. Consumers are excited with the new experience........ happy home-shopping!

SOCIAL BEHAVIOUR

The vociferous and just become powerful middle class that's started tasting all things good in life with some disposable income and all-round attention in the country, likes his new found freedom and western lifestyle and feels for his tribe members. He treads on the danger zone to maximize happiness & instant gratification. He doesn't like to be questioned on his choices and lifestyle. Unfortunately, the ugly faces lurk across the urban roads and waiting to pounce on the women, who have been constantly

> "Sentiments on faith, nationalism, ideology and language rule the heart more than the mind. Tweaking of the same, debates on medieval mind-set, archaic rituals and questioning of the same elicits strong and extreme reactions."

reduced to objects of desire and subjugation. These bestial creeps impose their manliness on the hapless girls. This also questions disturbingly on the basic flaw in our social education system and upbringing. Even babies are being abused physically. Lust has blinded many and the girls now refuse to trust any men.

In the race to modernity and with the negative influences from the West besides, clamour for power with the help of new found economic freedom, we forget our rich culture and traditions. The lines in between is getting blurred by the day. All age-old good practices are relegated as old style and regressive postures. Is progression antithesis to civilized norms?

There are several factors that need close examination to unravel the mysterious behaviour. Exhibitionism has become the style statement of the youth in public. Questioning this elicits negative barbs and the opposing party branded uncivilized and anti-feminism. At times, they exceed all forms of decency. Choice of dress defies the occasion. Unfortunately the Fraudian theory gets into act and the seething attraction to the opposite sex works sheepishly under the cloaked surface. The undercurrent of sexual adventurism breaks onto the surface with the least controlled libidos. Now the scene on the other side is equally baffling. Why every leg under a skirt is arousing manly passion? Is it looked upon as a challenge to the century old stronghold of the patriarch form of society? Are we men feeling threatened by the new age women and their new found freedom that we sneak into our primordial animal instinct to subjugate them?

Of course, there is no fear of law and state. The latter has miserably failed in managing its constitutional responsibilities. The politicians-businessmen nexus has pushed the middle class people and the marginalized bottom-of-the-pyramid in the society to the fringe and they get restless and revolt. Unfortunately, the majority remains indifferent and silent. We don't react unless it affects us. The daily urban scenes of accident victim lying unattended on the street are a common sight and are evident of this disturbing and growing psyche. We all have become so self-centred and myopic that such incidence only finds our indifferent stance and occasional tokenism support...more in style than sincerity.

Well, the morbid mind-set and one-dimensional analysis of issues disturbs me no end. But, everyone wants to sound politically correct and hence, diplomatic response. This buries the truth and we continue to tread on hypocrisy. Crimes thrive and we continue to debate endless.

Sentiments on faith, nationalism, ideology and language rule the heart more than the mind. Tweaking of the same, debates on medieval mind-set, archaic rituals and questioning of the same elicits strong and extreme reactions. Fundamentalism lurks its ugly heads in most religions and the civilization has been held to ransom. Barbaric killings of innocents make daily headlines today. The incessant incidents of such negative news have disturbingly made people indifferent to certain extent. Fear psychosis has gripped many and the saner voices got muffled in the act. Retaliations are often being justified by the opposing members. Eye for an eye has made all blind. Freedom of expression has been the biggest casualty. We have failed to agree to disagree. Intolerance and lack of respect for each other have punctured the social fabric. But in the race towards self-gratification and selfish goals in this world of consumerism have engineered great gulf between individuals. Today, we feel cocooned in our comfort zone. Unless directly affected, we prefer not to react. The friendly neighbourhood and rescuing Samaritans have sadly become extinct species. Humanitarian gesture has taken a beating. Only the self-serviced people with vested interest are roaming about with masks on to woe the targets. Once used, they are dumped by the roadside to suffer agonizing obscurity and shame. It is said to succeed, you must be selfish and trample others under the feet while climbing up the ladder of awards and recognition. Focus and determination are ought to be desired but the subjective interpretation dwells on the negativity and selfishness.

No wonder, even the corporate circle is besieged with stressed employees driven to utter dismay and despondency. After all at the end of the day, the bottom-line is the numbers! In the name of cost cutting and to remain competitive, value of time and effort are tossed out of the window. There is a paradigm shift in the employees' wage structure. The variable components outnumber the fixed. Only profit driven business rules the corridor of the corporate hegemony that throws human lives into deep uncertainty and uses the human resource as mere tools towards achieving their goal. Many an organization has turned into a sweat factory. Human beings are relegated to mere guinea pigs, ready to be dissected till they succumb to the pressure. When the chips are down, this glorified human resource becomes the first casualty and gets the boot at times, even denying them their legitimate dues.

Narcissism and instant gratification have been all pervasive as been witnessed in the social media. There are about 300 million photos are being posted daily on Facebook by its users. An analytical lens trained on the goings on in the Facebook would reveal this growing social behaviour that thrives on unabashed exhibitionism, extreme hedonism, mass endorsement, instant gratification and an untiring desire to speak on and express opinions on everything, even without domain expertise or with mere general knowledge and heresy. The issues that were considered taboos and against Indian tradition, culture and family values not too long ago, have been embraced blindly today in the name of development and advancing civilization. The resultant fallouts today have gripped the Indians with growing intolerance in relationships leading to more cases of divorce, overt sexual escapades and exhibitionism, rising obesity in epidemic proportion with unhealthy eating habits and a sedate lifestyle that is bordered more on unchecked and ever seducing consumerism. Stress filled life has consumed more lives today and our indifferent and selfish attitude have crumbled relationships.

Primary education has to be focused on by the educationists and the social scientists to inculcate all the good human values in a scientific manner and in line with the demands of the industry. Emotional quotient needs to be upped in the personality growth and development to surmount the challenges that the contemporary world is faced with. The growing up adult moves about with a baggage on and seldom evolves in the process. Good human values, humane qualities and discipline need to be injected into at the very beginning in the child and should be made an integral part of her growing up process. Investment at this initial stage of human growth would elicit a healthy return and the tomorrow's society would have better citizens.

Today we need Statesman, sane & free voice with objective analysis to stick its neck out and see the perspectives in true form and not with jaundiced eyes. Let's have some serious introspection. Before we become changed agents, let's first change ourselves and our mind-sets. We see what we want to, while we don't listen but engage the whole society in meandering arguments. The struggling by-lanes of our evolving civilization is decaying, giving way to morbid mind-sets and byzantine emotions. Let's rise and awake...we are still to be civilized. Materialistic advancement and economic freedom have altered the human-beings. We are less humane today and the animal within is threatening to overpower our sense & sensibilities. Beware; the creator didn't create us to annihilate the civilization by killing each other. Humanity must stand up today and be counted.

LEADERSHIP

Recently I told a group of leadership executives of Lions Club, Bangalore a simple but meaningful story that you may have heard before. I keep quoting it every time I have to speak on Leadership and being Responsible, Action oriented, to take control of the situation and get things going.

> *"Leadership and respect doesn't come from a business card. It is the character, courage, ethics, value systems and valour you embody that does the needful."*

It's the story of four people named Everybody, Somebody, Anybody and Nobody.

Here's the story, titled "Whose Job Is It, Anyway?"

This is a story about four people named Everybody, Somebody, Anybody and Nobody. There was an important job to be done and Everybody was sure that Somebody would do it. Anybody could have done it, but Nobody did it. Somebody got angry about that, because it was Everybody's job. Everybody thought Anybody could do it, but Nobody realized that Everybody wouldn't do it. It ended up that Everybody blamed Somebody when Nobody did what Anybody could have.

The story may be confusing but the message is clear: no one took responsibility so nothing got accomplished.

It's a story that plays out often in organizations and companies and on teams, even in our society—anywhere there is culture that lacks accountability.

Spontaneous response and reactions to Situations define a personality. Persons perceived to be timid and shy could turn heroes, exhibiting courage and tenacity while, visibly stronger and extroverts could chicken out, when summoned to take leadership.

But how do you get people to take responsibility for their work? Different things work in different situations, but here are some strategies that have proven to be effective.

1. Become a role model. You can't tell people what to do if you yourself aren't willing to hold yourself to the same level. If you want people to act responsibly, you have to be accountable. Your team and your company look to you for direction. Leadership is all about leading by example and the rest always fall in line.

2. Don't make assumptions. Don't assume that others know instinctively what to do and when to do it, or even what you expect from them. Before people can take responsibility for their work they require clear communication. The more you communicate, the better the results are likely to be.

3. Set the standard. If you expect excellence, it's up to you to set the standards for results and performance. Make each task or goal measurable and set it on a reasonable timeline so it's achievable. Give people a clear target and they'll work to reach it—and maybe even surpass it.

    Peter Drucker said, "Efficiency is doing things Right. Effectiveness is doing the Right things."

    Becoming the best version of yourself requires you to continuously edit your beliefs to upgrade and expand your identity.

4. Get the buy-in to go the distance. You need people to buy in and commit if you want to succeed. Each vision should be compelling; each goal should build toward the whole; each task should be laced with motivation. You need people to feel compelled, inspired and motivated to take responsibility. Hence, a gift of gab and a sense of humour help. Leadership is about taking everyone along – good, bad and the ugly...without compromising on core values.

5. Make regular check-ups. One of the biggest reasons people fall short is a lack of follow-through by leadership. Help people stay focused by setting up regular checkpoints—phone calls or meetings where everyone can communicate and catch up, staying focused on moving forward and being accountable. When people know there will be check-ups, they're less likely to procrastinate and more likely to hit their targets.

6. Provide support and training. Especially with a start-up or a new initiative, people are taking on projects or tasks that they've never faced before. Make sure everybody has the training and resources they need to be successful, and provide help in resolving any issues that may arise.

7. Encourage candour...being open, frank and honest. One of the worst things that can happen to a team is for people to feel uncomfortable discussing problems and expressing their honest opinions. Build a culture of candour so that people know it's the norm to tell the truth, even when it's difficult or awkward.

8. Concentrate on solutions and not only problems. If people are having problems or falling behind, expect them to come to you with possible solutions, not just the problems. Create an expectation that the first response to a problem is to start finding solutions.

9. Praise performance. Praise people for good results and be specific with your acknowledgment. Let them know what they did well and

how their work is affecting others. If they fall short, coach them privately and let them know how they can improve. And if their performance does not improve, also address this with meaningful consequences that have been explained ahead of time.

10. Leadership is Professional Knowledge and Professional Competence with Analytical Mind and Self Confidence. Ability to Think, be Decisive, be Responsible and be Accountable for all acts of omissions and commissions. Moral and Physical Courage are also necessary in different situations.

11. Self-Belief is important. If you think you can, you can do it. Risks have to be taken at times but one cannot take risks without convictions. If there is conviction in your eyes, you will sound confident and your followers/listeners/customers will believe you, will buy from you.

12. Popular Motivational Guru Shiv Khera said, "Winners don't do different things, they do things differently."

    To avoid having your team become Everybody, Somebody, Anybody and Nobody, commit to becoming the kind of leader who takes responsibility for your own life and leadership.

13. Lead from within: Don't let Anybody (or Everybody, Somebody or Nobody) stop you from doing what you need to do to create the kind of leadership and life you can be proud of.

I also quote another favourite of mine in the same context and that's the Pareto Principle of 80:20, which reasons that 20% of our Efforts produce 80% of the works as a result. Hence identifying and focusing on this 20% is very important, and we must prioritise it for the desired results and to be productive.

All great leaders throughout history share common characteristics and attributes that not only made them unique, but also helped leading great movements with ideas that were uncommon and less travelled.

These individuals were not born leaders; they developed leadership habits, moving out of their comfort zones and followed the inspiring example of those that came before them. They were committed to their visions and became Change Agents, Walking the Talks. History is replete with inspirational stories of several leaders in different fields and different walks of life from around the world: Mahatma Gandhi, Martin Luther King Jr., Nelson Mandela, Abraham Lincoln, Dr. APJ Abdul Kalam, Field Marshal Sam Manekshaw, Mountain Man Dashrath Manjhi, and several biblical heroes from all faiths.

Strong persons committed to a cause and espousing the same attracts the attention of others with similar minds, becoming the rallying points and thus centres of gravity that inspires others. Hence, leaders must identify their causes and stay committed with conviction. Followers will rally around the cause through the leaders. Remember, most people are always followers and leaders are always a handful few. Not all could have the courage and conviction with responsibility and accountability. Lead from the front, you will have people following you. When the raison d'atre finds resonance with others, you will have followers. Indomitable human spirits endure the journey hence; the leaders never give up while facing challenges.

Leadership and respect doesn't come from a business card. It is the character, courage, ethics, value systems and valour you embody that does the needful. A leader must be armed with knowledge, skills, intelligence, strategy, commitment and passion.

MIND-SET

"Watch your Thoughts, they become your Words;

Watch your Words, they become your Actions;

Watch your Actions, they become your Habits;

Watch your Habits, they become your Character;

Watch your Character; it becomes your Destiny."

> – Lao Tzu

"A sense of Pride and Ownership helps in rooting for a certain thing and pushing ahead to get it, own it, or improve it."

Your mind will always believe everything you tell it. Whatever you feed it with, will get you the same only. But when you are emotionally invested, you lose clarity.

In decision theory and general systems theory, a mind-set is a set of assumptions, methods, or notions held by one or more people or groups of people. A mind-set can also be seen as arising out of a person's world view or philosophy of life.

You only limit yourself by your imagination. Your attitude decides your altitude. "You will never know your limits until you push yourself to them", so said Amy Rees Anderson. Don't be afraid to fail, be afraid not to try. Because, there is no failure, you either win or learn. The difference between who you are and who you want to be is what you do. So, one must get into action and take the first step to move. The distance between your dreams and reality is called action. To walk, you have to take a step forward and continuation of this becomes your walk to moving forward, your journey towards your dreams and wishes.

We all have this tendency to simply fretting over the absence of something desired and thus, blaming all others except looking within and rising up to get counted. More often than not, we expect someone else to do it rather than us taking it up and getting done. Inertia, indifference, indecisiveness, and absence of ownership prevent us from getting into action. It's not just self-doubt and all that aforesaid but our mind-set which limits our imagination. Just look around and analyse all that's happening or the absence of it, you will conclude on this unfortunate common human trait. This is such a common disease that infects most of us, reducing us to mere grumblers, indulging in negativity and living in denial. This is the biggest impediment for progress and growth.

"The world as we have created it is a process of our thinking. It cannot be changed without changing our thinking."

– Albert Einstein

A sense of Pride and Ownership helps in rooting for a certain thing and pushing ahead to get it, own it, or improve it.

Complaining, whining, criticizing are negative mindsets that don't allow us to get into action to improve upon anything, as required. If we decide to do something and are determined, all challenges turn opportunities.

Explaining about the Atomic Habits, James Clear says that "habits are the compound interest of self-improvement. Getting 1% better every day counts for a lot in the long run." Expanding this further he opines,

"Becoming better version of yourself requires you to continuously edit your beliefs to upgrade and expand your identity."

Change requires adjustment. Adjustment of ideas approaches and sometimes even of heart, but not of hope, values or necessarily vision. When the mind is trapped in negativity; happiness, joy, love and creativity become the casualties and we fail to evolve further.

Everything we want in life is waiting for us in two zones: outside of our comfort zones and inside of our effort zone. Courage is your personal power, your inner strength. When utilized, mountains can be scaled. Aristotle once said, "Pleasure in the job puts perfection in the work." One should enjoy her work and the same will be enjoyable. Emphasizing on the mindsets, Elon Musk says, "When something is important enough, you do it even if the odds are not in your favour." Questioning our assumptions would clear our minds and would help us pushing towards action in a positive manner. If others similar to me could do it, why can't I? -should be the question we must ask ourselves always.

> *"Complaining, whining, criticizing are negative mindsets that don't allow us to get into action to improve upon anything, as required. If we decide to do something and are determined, all challenges turn opportunities."*

There is another interesting facet to human characteristics, especially seen in our country. For example, when certain State government made it mandatory for the 2-wheeler riders to wear Helmets, many people resisted, offering excuses of all sorts but with the passage of time, settled down with it. Isn't it a mindset issue? Then there is a positive and negative mindset. Most of us whine and blame the government for not doing this, not doing that. And there is a bunch of youngsters called, The Ugly Indians, who volunteer to paint the flyovers and public walls beautifully with murals and graphics. And there is this Pothole Raja Volunteers in Bangalore, who patch up potholes with tar, when requested. There are several responsible and concerned citizens across India, who do up the work, instead of stay complaining. Such acts prove that, there are no limits to what you can accomplish, except the limits you place on your own thinking.

In order to take India forward and to command respect as Indians, shedding inertia, deserting negativity and changing in our mind-sets are highly desired.

Veteran Ad Guru and popular Lyricist Mr. Prasoon Joshi during his address to the executives of SAP Labs at Bangalore few summers ago said the following:

"What's the sign of ageing? Getting bogged down by limitations. You have learnt so much that the mind tells you, it can't be done. Why do you think every civilization believes in youth, because, youngsters are not aware of limitations. He/she always asks: Why not? And Children are completely unaware of limitations. They paint the sky green and ask why can't it be green? As adults we get worried when they do that. During the making of Taare Zameen Par I explored the world of children a lot. I discovered that adults are lazy. But a child's mind is always ticking. Observe a child and an adult looking at a tree — the child's eye is roving; it doesn't stop for a moment. The child is 'looking' at the tree. Whereas the adult has already decided that he is looking at the tree. That's the difference between a child's eye and an adult's. Never let the child's eye in you go blind or die, when it does, innovation in you dies."

LIFE SKILLS & VALUES

Life is a beautiful journey that throws several challenges in its path. When skilled with the variables and understanding each new experience that come our way, it helps us managing the difficulties. But not too many of us possess this and often found struggling with despair. Life is not always happy-go-lucky and hunky-dory for all. With the Nature's inevitable

> *"Like professional skills are required to enhance career, life skills will help tide over challenges and control emotions. Values are the guiding factors that add substance and self-respect."*

inequalities, each of us has to experience the same journey differently but mostly, proportionate to our acts of omissions and commissions, following the cause-effect theory. Decision making and problem solving are unavoidable moments that often define the course of our journey and the quality of life that we could follow subsequently. Life skills are abilities for adaptive and positive behaviour that enable humans to deal effectively with the demands and challenges of life. When we simply go with the flow, we experience varied moments, ups and downs, hope and despair, happiness and sorrow, more often than not an uncontrolled drive. Experiences do teach us but not before pushing us to go through the upheavals. Therefore is the necessity of learning life skills for a relatively smoother path in this journey for happier outcomes.

"The greatest discovery of my generation is that a human being can alter his life by altering his attitudes" says William James (Psychologist)

Psychosocial competence is a person's ability to deal effectively with the demands and challenges of everyday life. We acquire professional skills, while during our life's journey we learn life skills. But conscious efforts to learn help us dealing with situations better. Many of us have intelligence. We enhance knowledge with education and training but emotions manage most of our actions hence, need regulated and controlled emotions.

There are many such skills, but core life skills include the ability to coping with emotions and the resulting stress, critical thinking & decision making, effective communication and accepting failure as a learning process and not as the end of this world.

The Ten core Life Skills as laid down by WHO are:

1. Self-awareness
2. Empathy
3. Critical thinking
4. Creative thinking
5. Decision making
6. Problem Solving
7. Effective communication
8. Interpersonal relationship
9. Coping with stress
10. Coping with emotion

Home is the first school for everyone and parents have a responsibility to teach life skills, mostly by engaging their kids in the daily household works and become the example for them in everything. Children are great observers and fast learners. Parents have to behave responsibly and help creating an educative and positive atmosphere, inculcating good values and practices. Over indulgence could spoil them and indifference could dishearten. Primary schools also should do similarly, because after home and parents, children spend maximum time there, learning all that are being imparted to them by the teachers. This way, their foundations could be built strongly for a safer and smoother voyage ahead in life. Family is the closest circle around you. It gives a sense of comfort and foundation.

"Though comparison is obvious yet it generates various emotions, negatives mostly. Absence of knowledge and such shortcomings and imperfections induce us to defend ourselves and even justify, thereby closing doors for learning and improvement."

Friend circle is another close circle that influences you as much. It is important to be surrounded by positive energy which ultimately defines and moulds you in a particular shape. Hence, your energy should also be positive always while your thinking should be progressive.

Of late, we have been hearing very disturbing news about how children and the youth are snuffing their lives out, unable to face challenges and in failure. Rejections and defeats should be faced chin up and not to be treated as the end of the world. Remember, when one door closes, more open up. We just need to have perseverance, staying positive, without allowing our self-confidence to get affected in any manner possible. Wallowing in self-pity and sulking long on the challenges during the difficult times would only make us suffer more. Acting timely on the available opportunities and finding solutions could only help tiding over the surging waves of negative emotions.

Frustrations creep in and confidence wobbles when in short supply of certain knowledge and skill. So, in order to overcome this, one needs to soar up the shortcomings within and replenish the minds and hearts with relevant knowledge and skills. Learning is a continuous process and there is no end to this. At the same time, we must accept that imperfection is natural and inequality is also a common phenomenon in this planet. Though comparison is obvious yet it generates various emotions, negatives mostly. Absence of knowledge and such shortcomings and imperfections induce us to defend ourselves and even justify, thereby closing doors for learning and improvement. If not addressed suitably, it remains an uncovered sink-hole, which could expand further into a larger crater, forcing us to trip over and fall. Someone rightly said that this modern world does have human beings but humanity is missing.

Emotional Quotient (EQ) helps us managing and overcoming various human emotions and thus, facing challenges better.

All the ills afflicting our society and our behaviours today are simply in the absence of values, which is a prime factor in the growth and progress of any civilization. Values and principles help refining and restructuring our clumsy minds, eliciting positive thoughts, offering strength and courage to face the challenges in life. There is deep meaning and profound thoughts behind values and principles. Following them help leading a disciplined life that would give peace and self-respect. Everything in our lives need to work within a boundary, moving beyond it invites challenges. We must know where to draw the line in everything that we do and think of. Acting within the boundary, as prescribed by the civilized society, helps in managing the same rather smoothly and with less hassles. Values define this boundary and teach us to act within it. Over indulgence creates all trouble.

"Relationships are crumbling and intolerance growing while mutual respect, especially for the seniors is missing. No society is civilised if value systems are ignored. One doesn't develop values just by being religious. Conscience plays a major role in shaping up minds, instilling discipline."

With the passage of time, men taste more freedom and thus, explore all desires and vicars and willingly trespass into the prohibited zones, as much out of curiosity as using his new found liberty, committing mistakes in the process. In the process of growing up, human beings leave behind their innocence, donning a complex attitude.

Traditionally, Indian society had been espousing and following value systems, which could be seen especially among the art and cultural communities with the much celebrated "Guru-Shishya Parampara" (Teacher-Disciple Traditions) and respecting the elders and teachers has been an inseparable social ethos. With the onset of the 21st century, the free global economy brought in crass consumerism and over indulgence, pushing behind the value system. Hedonism, over-indulgence and crass consumerism overpowered our minds and absence of value systems, pushed us into loss, pain and sufferings. Negativity envelops our confused minds and frustrations and anger leads to depression. A mere glance around most families, our society and several institutions, mirror the glaring absence of values and ethics. The Millennials may not understand this as they have stepped into such a world that is bereft of values and principles at every step in life. And we rue this today. Relationships are crumbling and intolerance growing while mutual respect, especially for the seniors is missing. No society is civilised if value systems are ignored. One doesn't develop values just by being religious. Conscience plays a major role in shaping up minds, instilling discipline. Values emerge from that. A man will be a mere living creature without having conscience and values.

As your definition of success changes, so do your personal values. This is why keeping in touch with your values is a lifelong exercise. You should continuously revisit this, especially if you start to feel unbalanced... and you can't quite figure out why. Some of life's decisions are really about determining what you value most. When multiple options seem reasonable, leading perhaps to confusion and dilemma, it's helpful and comforting to rely on your values – and use them as a guiding force to take you in the right direction.

Ask yourself what do you want at the end of the day...Peace? So be it. If you value health, you will maintain balanced food and healthy life style. If you value relationship, you will nurture and care for them, no matter how much differences you could be experiencing at times. Plenty of excuses are available, if you are looking for one. But will that help moving things further, offering peace and contentment?

Ego, ambition and vested interests push us to find excuses and feel negative in everything. When will we love one another if we become judgmental?

Today, consumers are changing, the approach to marketing is changing, and technology is changing fast. You will need to upgrade and learn on a continuous basis.

Communication is much underrated. People think that it is merely command over a language and mastering the same. But it is much more and much beyond that, including listening and absorbing while understand the context, the domain and the audiences it is targeted to. Of course, a compelling storytelling would work wonder for you always...how persuasive you are and how focused as well. It always helps to be on top of the situation at hand though challenges offer them in different ways and handling each needs different techniques and approach.

Like professional skills are required to enhance career, life skills will help tide over challenges and control emotions. Values are the guiding factors that add substance and self-respect. Lifelong learning is no longer optional, it's necessary. Procrastination is a very comfortable zone. Getting out of the comfort zone is the biggest crossroad that people face. Successful serial entrepreneur, Ronnie Screwvala says, "The one good thing about habits is that they have been challenged during the pandemic for everyone. A habit should always be questioned, because there's a sense of comfort with routine, and it doesn't challenge you."

CELEBRATING WOMEN

———•◯•———

The universe and this world have progressed, so are the lives of the human beings living within but some mind-sets remained stuck in the time warp zone. Even in this 21st Century, there are several men, who continue to dwell in the feudalism. The outer manifestation could exhibit a pseudo egalitarian view but the undercurrent emotions are unable to accept the women as equal partners. Either jealousy for the better-half or the domineering machismo,

> "A mutual respect society creates a support ecosystem and women should shed their veils of all social constraints and hypocrisy to establish their own identity with dignity and self-respect."

rule the relationship. Many educated working men with working spouses have this uneasy feeling in between. Men still wish his lady to be a coy caretaker. Many working women either are sacrificing and compromising their careers and ambitions or rebelling against. The tension continues affecting several couples and their families. Women still are struggling to have their choices and decisions. The paternalistic society shackles the freedom and the women fight on.

The other side of the story unfolds the hyper ambitious women, shirking family responsibilities in pursuance of hedonistic pleasure, unbridled freedom and career ambitions. Many married working ladies even don't wish to be biological mothers to rear up children. There are others who with their boundless freedom, try to manipulate men's emotions while skirting family responsibilities. Thus the troubled social milieu and mutual aggression, resulting in several breakups and disintegration.

Men and the women are the most beautiful creations of Nature. They must complement each other rather than competing with. Family value systems coupled with the sacred notion of respecting each other while according individual spaces, would put them on equal footing. World needs the gracious presence of the women and their inherent natural strength of multitasking coupled with the genetically soothing nature of love and compassion to make this world liveable in peace. Society would do itself a favour by encouraging them without strings attached and the men folks should offer space and support for mutual growth and happiness. Woman is beyond flesh and blood, she is the epitome of love and strength. A civilised society must know how to respect its women.

It is also equally important that women encourage, support and inspire each other. A mutual respect society creates a support ecosystem and women should shed their veils of all social constraints and hypocrisy to establish their own identity with dignity and self-respect. Women empowerment will remain hollow if gender bias continues to be an issue in countries like India. There have been several stories of indomitable women spirit, breaking the glass ceilings that could inspire the lesser mortals and the ones struggling to stick their necks out in the humdrum of social cauldrons. These women could be the role models to empower other women, uplifting their spirits and giving wings to their dreams and aspirations.

Let's raise a toast to all our beautiful ladies and take pride in having them with us. It is empathy and not sympathy that our women need. But more than that is to respect them. Let's celebrate their presence every day. Together WE Can.

Happy Women's Day...Every Day.

BE CONTENT BUT DREAM ALONG...

Appreciate what you have but don't restrict your dreams. Contentment will give peace and dream will keep you going. Ironical it is that human-beings are intrigued with. But the truth is, both are necessary for a peaceful growth.

"Ironical it is that without aspirations and attempting at improving, one cannot grow. In today's world, especially in the professional sphere, scaling up greater heights is a must have desire and smart planning and hardworking only ensure this."

The trappings of consumerism are antithesis to contentment and men get sucked into this whirlpool of insatiable urge to have more. Gautam Buddha said, "Happiness will never come to those who fail to appreciate what they already have." Gratitude is the key to happiness and abundance in your life. Focus on what you have and you will find you will attract more of it. He further said, "Pain is certain, suffering is optional." We all experience pain as human beings. But it is our attachment to that pain that causes us suffering. You can make the choice to end your suffering, right now, by accepting what is. Change your thoughts; it will change your life. Success is not the destination but a journey. Comparison is only healthy if it inspires you to do better. Desires and wants are many but need is few. Hedonism multiply our desires and we crave for all that we don't have but wish to possess and the race continue unabated. In our society, material possession often decides one's social status and image, though not necessarily could establish one's superiority by any means. It's a pseudo perception that men invariably fall for and keep accumulating material possessions, which is a bottomless pit and a never ending process. This of course doesn't mean one should only maintain an ascetic life, characterized by severe self-discipline and abstention from all forms of indulgence. But the question should be, where to and when to stop in this indulgent spree?

A man having a top end Jaguar fancies a private jet. Someone with a less fancied car rues his inability to have the Jaguar. The one who cycles around daily cribs about not having a bike or a car but realises the false vanity when comes across someone on the wheel chair, without legs. We human-beings always grumble and carry a sense of loss and deprivation, when we don't possess what others have and we desire for. But while looking around us, we see several people without what even we have, but enjoying themselves and never complaining or comparing with others. They are content but making effective use of what they have with them, working hard to improve life and career. Every pain gives a lesson and every lesson changes a person.

> *"Success is not the destination but the journey that doesn't end ever. Stagnancy stifles growth. The race to reach to the top is the manifestation of an aspirational soul. Consistency transforms average into excellence."*

Ironical it is that without aspirations and attempting at improving, one cannot grow. In today's world, especially in the professional sphere, scaling up greater heights is a must have desire and smart planning and hardworking only ensure this. It's perceived as an absolute negative if one's position doesn't improve gradually. Change is constant and one has to adapt to the same to stay relevant and grow. It's advised to dream big and pursue the same to transform it to reality. It's that dream which doesn't allow us to sleep but pushes us up always to improve and achieve. Success is not the destination but the journey that doesn't end ever. Stagnancy stifles growth. The race to reach to the top is the manifestation of an aspirational soul. Consistency transforms average into excellence.

History is replete with stories of luminaries attributing much of their genius to the many hours they spent lost in their mind. Reflective thinking as a critical component of being an effective teacher, works in ideating. A healthy amount of daydreaming that allows the mind to wander, along with reflection, induces non-linear connections to form, helping the mind to look through a new lens and indulge productively in thought experiments. Active Reflection is an important and routine part of teaching and it does help a lot to improve professional practice.

You are in your current situation because you have decided to be there. You have made the individual choices and decisions that have gotten you to your current place in life. If you want to go somewhere else or be someone else, it is totally up to you to make the choices and decisions today that will eventually get you there. And there are no limits. Brian Tracy said, "Dream big. There are no limitations to how good you can become or how high you can rise except the limits you put on yourself."

THE LAST WORD

—◦◯◦—

Employee Management

Robin has been working since last three years in this reputed company as a senior management professional in the Corporate Business Development. He has surmounted the challenges that come along the job and has been quite successful at that. Dedicated and sincere to the core, he goes about his assignment diligently and proactively working along with his team. He motivates and leads his team always from the front. He has not only established his company in the market but also wins several large businesses. He is quite popular in the company and commands respect in the industry for his leadership, success and professionalism with a human touch. But he feels a void within and is not happy with the ways in the company. He is denied any special incentive or promotion. Quite inexplicably, he finds many around him inching ahead every year by some means. This not only intrigues him but also demoralizes. Every year he just goes through the annual appraisal process rather mechanically. On a large project proposal he differs with the top management and logically objects to the strategy followed. Weeks on, he argues for his strategy with support from his team at the ground. Management doesn't buy his logic and he along with his team struggles to manage it with the prospect. He predicts losing the project and it comes true subsequently. The management turns around and blames him. There ensued an argument and on a feat of rage, the management leadership asks him to quit. Crestfallen, he pleads but to no avail. His sincere hard work goes down the drain. Seeing the outcome, the team backtracks though grumbles in private. The management gets a replacement and the show goes on.

The narration could easily find echo with several. Analysts, Business Management and HR Professionals analyse and debate. Several theories would be espoused and fault noted. But, the 'loser' cringes alone in private corner. He moves along and perhaps joins another organization. The fault line stays put.

Well, this is just an anecdote from a private corporate professional that occurs every day in some place or other with someone or the other. Speakers rattle about theories and debate in seminars and through journals. Various management theories are bandied about but history repeats!

The industrial age had led to a control paradigm, entrenching a "leadership by position" mentality. This ensue a lack of commitment or emotional connection by the detached workforce, who always viewed the employers as an exploiter and hence, lacked trust.

The Information Age or Knowledge worker in the Age of the Knowledge Economy has replaced the 'carrot & stick' of the Industrial Age, ushering in "leadership is a choice", empowering them in the process. In the new paradigm, the greatest asset in any organization is its people. With their regular contribution at the lower and middle levels could significantly impact with greater effect and leverage, bringing in greater change throughout the organization.

The maturing world has transformed the previously exclusive authority to empower the entire class.

Various skill improving tools today aim at the data analytics and problem solving characteristics among the workers. Driven by customer requirement, value additions are encouraged through cost effective innovations. Today, technology is invariably interlinked with the business to benefit the end users. Hence, the focus is on the market and the consumers. The technocrats need to talk the language of business and be business savvy. The distinction between the techies and the business professionals has blurred and the gulf bridged.

Several scientific tools and practices have been designed and imparted to the employees to enhance their skills, better performance in the job and even help advancing career.

It's held universally that human resource is the strength of an organization and they need to be trained, nurtured and kept happy to yield the desired result. HRD along with the L&D teams go through imparting trainings and introducing several measures keeping pace with various management theories and practices. Attrition rate continues north ward. Is it just compensation, promotion and incentives that motivate the employees? How much of the human element responsible and plays an ignored role in this rising phenomena? This is equally experienced in the highly professional as well as family run business houses the world over. The scenario definitely hinges more on the latter. Indian Infrastructure industry is mainly managed by family run management and invariably, the scenario remains similar all through.

Stories from the earlier world are replete with tales of respectable coexistence within organizations. There used to be an emotional connection among the workforce, the employers (the Masters) and the organization. Instances of unflinching loyalty, unquestionable integrity and deep emotional bonding – the incredulous stuff of folklore, were in existence. With the onset of Industrial Age, the conflict and social strife raised its ugly head creating an unbridged gap between the workers and the industrialists. Deficit of trust, accumulated greed, insatiable hedonistic consumerism and absence of loyalty vitiated the present knowledge economy beyond repair. Employee engagement drives are being introduced and put in practice but the 'heart' is missing from the mechanical exercise. The one dimensional 'only for benefit' mind-set pervaded the atmosphere making each person indifferent and detached. The gulf of trust stands enlarged and thus, beyond repair.

The situation has drifted to the extreme. There also have been disturbing reports of exiting employees denied of their legitimate dues illegally by some companies. Muted stories of disgruntled employees joining hands to drag the management into the court of law make for hushed office corner gossip. There have been several such inglorious instances of exploitation that have gone unreported. Absence of social protection and lingering legal processes have deterred employees in pursuing the matter but that have only embolden the unscrupulous elements at the cost of innocent lives.

Well, these are some of the fallouts of organizational manipulation and labour exploitation but the other side of the coin also paints another story of restless and disloyal employees. Millions of hard-earned dollars/ rupees are being spent for long towards the development and enhancing of employees' skillsets through various trainings and workshops, at the time of induction and during the tenure. Quitting for greener pastures and 'better opportunities', leaves the management in doldrums, rendering the efforts futile. The RoI draws negative and growing competition with pressure on costing/pricing makes it stressful and at times unviable for the project. Job hopping has become the norm these days in the private sector.

Learned and highly experienced professionals have authored their articles which are very insightful. Most of them painstakingly elaborate on various management theories and professional practices. Several have substantiated its efficacy with anecdotes laced with irrefutable statistics. Will such management theories and professional practices yield the desired results and arrest the disturbingly growing attrition rate in business organizations? Is there a human element that needs to be brought under the lens for a psycho-analytical study of human behaviour in the contemporary social context that could shed light better and could perhaps unveil the story that lies buried under? Do we have diagnostic questions that explore how the employees really feel? Does it create shared expectations through stakeholder analysis? Does it encourage a self-assessment support system or puts the words in the mouth to go along the expected lines? Does it balance between the employee's needs with the demands of the organization? Do we deal with just the 'content' issues or 'above the surface' in the iceberg metaphor or 'process' related issues (below the surface) to deal with human reactions, politics, resistance, fear etc.? Is the communication from the top always without allowing or with just tokenism through the HR muffle voices of dissent, discouraging questioning? Is there an inclusive growth strategy in place or just the crème-de-la-crème affair all the way? Several such questions go begging. In some places, employees are overly pampered during hey days and when the chips are down; they are the first to get the boot. An organization is the sum of its employees but the organization (read as Promoters) prevails over always.

THANK YOU DEAR READER

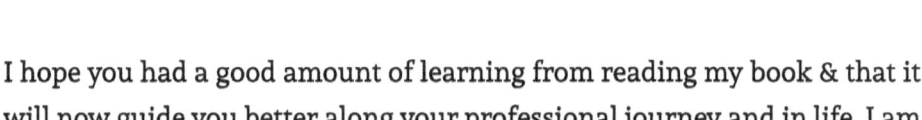

I hope you had a good amount of learning from reading my book & that it will now guide you better along your professional journey and in life. I am very happy that you have read this to the very last word. Appreciate your time.

One last thing...

If you wish to share your thoughts about the book or anything related to this, you can reach out to me via:

E-mail: pkpani@yahoo.com

LinkedIn: https://www.linkedin.com/in/pranabpani

Facebook: https://www.facebook.com/pranabpani

Twitter: @pkpani1

Please take good care of yourself & this beautiful Earth.

Best wishes,

Pranab K. Pani